The Secret

Of

Church Growth

THE SECRET

OF

CHURCH GROWTH

First Chinese Baptist Church
Los Angeles, California

THE SECRET OF CHURCH GROWTH

Author: Dr. Timothy Lin
Translator: Ruth Wai-Hing Taniguchi

Chinese Edition
教會增長的秘訣
(Chiao-hui tsêng-chang tê mi-chüeh)
© 1983 by China Evangelical Seminary Press

Scripture quotations are from the New American Standard
Bible, © 1960, 1962, 1963, 1968, 1971, 1972, 1973, 1975, 1977 by
The Lockman Foundation. Used by permission.

ISBN   0-945304-01-3
Library of Congress Catalog Card Number
Printed in the United States of America

In memory of my late wife

Grace Wu Lin

whose life and love had been a source of

constant inspiration to me.

PREFACE

"O taste and see that the LORD is good..." (Ps. 34:8). Dr. Timothy Lin has tasted and has found the Lord to be good. His life in the Lord has been rich and deep, especially in the understanding (not just the knowledge) of the Word and the person of God. The Lord has been exceptionally gracious towards him in the illumination of His Word and His way. This, integrated with a full and still active life of service which encompasses over 60 years of experiences as a preacher, pastor, professor, scholar and seminary president, gives Dr. Lin a unique and insightful perspective into the Church.

From the same verse comes one of the author's favorite illustrations, that of an excellent orange. In order to experience the juicy sweetness of the fruit, one must bite into and taste that fruit. Dr. Lin has experienced the contents of this book. He has, over the decades, tested these principles in his own life and in his churches. None are theoretical or hypothetical. All have been tested in the laboratory of life. He has found them to be practical, workable and blessed of the Lord.

I too have tasted them personally. Having been taught and having applied these principles (as a layman and as a pastor), their effectiveness is evidenced in the qualitative and quantitative changes of many lives. Through a church and Sunday school which practiced the contents of this book, I came to know and receive the Lord Jesus as Savior. Years later this practice yielded the fruit of the salvations of my own father and mother. This blessing has been further multiplied as I witnessed my father train and serve as a Sunday school teacher, impacting the lives of his students and contributing to the growth of the church.

I therefore invite you to, with a quote from this book, "Please give it a try!" Read this book carefully. Think about its contents deeply. Finally, apply it studiously. Taste and see.

Pastor Jackson Lau
Pharm. D., M. Div.
FCBC, San Gabriel

Los Angeles, California
June, 1992

FOREWORD

Church growth has, in the past some twenty years, held a significant position in Christian literature and documents, as well as in sharing, sermons, prayers and hymns. Such an emphasis on church growth is a good indication of most Christians' concern for the expansion of God's kingdom. But, what has ultimately transpired in the vicissitude of time?

Even in prominent churches, prayer meeting attendance still consists of the usual few. Be it a workshop or a seminar, oftentimes, the only ones present are the few faithful seniors. What has gone wrong?

The Bible has rightly said, "But let all things be done properly and in an orderly manner" (1 Cor. 14:40). The ancient Chinese book of wisdom, Ta-hsüeh 大學　(The Great Learning) has also said,

> All things have roots and branches, and all affairs have beginnings and endings. The person, who is able to set the proper priority, truly understands the teachings of the great learning.

Ta-hsüeh has further emphasized that:

> With the roots in a chaotic turmoil, healthy branches can never be developed. No person will grossly neglect what is of crucial importance, yet painstakingly care for what is of trivial importance.

Anyone who abandons the roots in pursuit of the branches or upsets the order of proper priority, will surely find it difficult to succeed. Spiritual things are likewise the same!

Organizing seminars on church growth and studying documents and literature about this topic are, of course, valuable and helpful in attaining church growth. However, the assumption that church growth will come about by merely analyzing the external factors and recommending techniques and procedures is unrealistic! These are at best techniques trying to cope with the symptoms of a problem, rather than principles striving to cure the roots of the problem. To cure the roots of the problem, we have to find answers from the Bible. It is my prayer that the principles suggested in this book will be helpful to God's Church. These principles are based upon my few decades of pastoring bestowed by our gracious Lord.

More than 10,000 copies of the Chinese edition were sold within a brief period of time after the first print, and it has been reprinted again and again. Many churches have used this book as a guideline for church growth, and some have even used it as an outline for training church leaders. For this, I humbly thank our Lord! May the Head of the Church, who has revealed to us His promises and required conditions, bless all who are willing to fulfill these conditions, that they may enjoy the realization of His promises. Amen!

This English version is the result of the tireless effort and dedicated love of the following brothers and sisters. I would like to express my special appreciation to sister Ruth Taniguchi for translating and editing the book. I would also like to thank Penny Wong, Mike Taniguchi, Eugene Wilkerson, Charles Lee, Hannah Lee, David Shigekawa, Gordon Yee and Pastor Jackson Lau for proof-reading. A special thanks is also extended to Harold Wong for word processing and Marshall Kwong for designing the book cover. May God's name be glorified!

List of Abbreviations

Gen. - Genesis
Ex. - Exodus
Lev. - Leviticus
Num. - Numbers
Deut. - Deuteronomy
Josh. - Joshua
Judg. - Judges
Ruth - Ruth
1 Sam. - 1 Samuel
2 Sam. - 2 Samuel
1 Kin. - 1 Kings
2 Kin. - 2 Kings
1 Chr. - Chronicles
2 Chr. - Chronicles
Ezra - Ezra
Neh. - Nehemiah
Esth. - Esther
Job - Job
Ps. - Psalms
Prov. - Proverbs
Eccl. - Ecclesiastes
Song - Song of Solomon
Is. - Isaiah
Jer. - Jeremiah
Lam. - Lamentations
Ezek. - Ezekiel
Dan. - Daniel
Hos. - Hosea
Joel - Joel
Amos - Amos
Obad. - Obadiah
Jon. - Jonah
Mic. - Micah

Nah. - Nahum
Hab. - Habakkuk
Zeph. - Zephaniah
Hag. - Haggai
Zech. - Zechariah
Mal. - Malachi
Matt. - Matthew
Mark - Mark
Luke - Luke
John - John
Acts - Acts
Rom. - Romans
1 Cor. - 1 Corinthians
2 Cor. - 2 Corinthians
Gal. - Galatians
Eph. - Ephesians
Phil. - Philippians
Col. - Colossians
1 Thess. - 1 Thessalonians
2 Thess. - 2 Thessalonians
1 Tim. - 1 Timothy
2 Tim. - 2 Timothy
Titus - Titus
Philem. - Philemon
Heb. - Hebrews
Jas. - James
1 Pet. - 1 Peter
2 Pet. - 2 Peter
1 John - 1 John
2 John - 2 John
3 John - 3 John
Jude - Jude
Rev. - Revelation

CONTENTS

1

THE SECRET OF CHURCH GROWTH

"The secret things belong to the LORD our God," the Bible tells us, "but the things revealed belong to us and to our sons forever..." (Deut. 29:29). Yes, it is true! Secret things, indeed, belong to God, and He alone can reveal them. Just as He has promised,

> I proclaim to you new things from this time,
> Even hidden things which you have not known.
> (Is. 48:6)

He did in fact reveal to Daniel, for instance, "the profound and hidden things" (Dan. 2:22). And, in the same manner, He allowed Paul to hear the "inexpressible words, which a man is not permitted to speak" (2 Cor. 12:4).

I am deeply convinced that the content of this book has been gradually revealed to me by God over the span of some twenty years. All the principles mentioned herein are applicable and offer immediate results to our daily Christian lives. Application of these principles is as effortless as what Han Yü 韓愈 , a famous Chinese man of letters, once said, "It is as easy as four horses drawing a light carriage along a familiar road!"

May God enlighten us, and help us to "be strong and very courageous; [and] be careful to do according to" the principles He has taught us. If our Christian lives reflect this, then we can be very sure that church growth will come without much difficulty.

In The Old Testament

In the Old Testament times, the prerequisite for God's people to be blessed was to have God's presence. Such a principle is clearly demonstrated through the lives of various Old Testament spiritual giants.

A good example is Isaac. During his sojourn in the land of the Philistines, he was able to reap a hundredfold amidst racial discrimination and persecution because of God's presence. His prosperity was so great that even the king of the

2

Philistines solemnly said to him, "We see plainly that the LORD has been with you...," and subsequently requested a covenant with him (Gen. 26:3, 13, 26-28).

Another example is Jacob, who, while living in Laban's house as a dependent, was repeatedly exploited and had his wages changed ten times. Yet, because of God's presence, he was able to father a multitude of children and return home with great abundance (Gen. 28:15; 30:27; 31:42).

The same is true with Joseph. Having been sold to a foreign land as a slave and wronged with false accusations and unjust imprisonment, Joseph was ultimately able to cast away prison garb for fine linen and rule over the whole land of Egypt. The sole reason for such a dramatic outcome was that God's presence was with him (Gen. 39:2-6, 20-23).

Joshua conquered all the kings in Canaan one by one (Deut. 31:23; Josh. 1:5); Samuel received the special blessing that God would let "none of his words fail" (1 Sam. 3:19); and King David enjoyed prosperity in all his ways (1 Sam. 18:14). The triumph of these spiritual giants was a simple result of this secret—they had God's presence!

In short, if we want our church to grow, if we want to reap a hundredfold, and if we want to prosper, be respected and trusted instead of being scoffed at, we must have the presence of God.

In The New Testament

The importance of having God's presence became even more evident during the Early Church Period. After the departure of God's glory from the holy temple during the time of Ezekiel (Ezek. 9:3; 10:4, 18-19; 11:23-24), the Jews realized that God had truly forsaken them (Ezek. 8:6, 12; 9:9). In expressing their grievances to God, they often said,

> They say to me all day long, "Where is your God?" (Ps. 42:3,10)

> O God, why hast Thou rejected us forever? (Ps. 74:1)

> Yet Thou hast rejected us....(Ps. 44:9)

Their prayers were:

> Awake, do not reject us forever. (Ps. 44:23)

> O God of hosts, turn again now. (Ps. 80:14)

Throughout the whole Intertestamental Period, devout Jews were waiting for God's return to their midst (Luke 2:25, 38; 23:51).

Now, at the dawn of the Early Church Period, there suddenly came from heaven a noise, and there appeared to them tongues as of fire which enabled the apostles to speak in other languages. In all the excitement, the Jews heard Peter preach that God cared for them. They then realized that their

God who had forsaken them had once again returned to them. Consequently, three thousand people became Christians on that day.

A few days after this incident, a man lame from birth, whom people laid daily at the gate of the holy temple to beg for money, was healed through the name of Jesus the Nazarene. This man entered the holy temple walking, leaping and praising God! Such a miracle once again substantiated the fact that God had come to them (ref. Acts 3:1-11). For the same reason, right after Peter's second testimony, many believed, and the number of new converts (just men alone) came to about five thousand.

God's presence was further demonstrated through His holiness. After Ananias and Sapphira met sudden death because they lied to God, "great fear came upon the whole church, and upon all who heard of these things." As a result, "all the more believers in the Lord, multitudes of men and women, were constantly added to their number" (Acts 5:11, 14).

Even when believers were persecuted and scattered all over Judea and Asia Minor following the stoning of Stephen, God's presence followed them wherever they went. As a result, "a large number who believed turned to the Lord" (Acts 11:19-21).

Thus, the Holy Spirit clearly tells us that the secret of church growth during the Early Church Period was God's presence, and that the work of the Holy Spirit was sure evidence of His presence. The

Church of the last days must have the presence of God if she wants to grow, or all efforts will be futile.

The Required Conditions

The presence of God is a promise from God, and a grace He has prepared for His Church as well as for individual Christians. God's promise and grace are objective realities. In order to change an objective reality into a subjective blessing—that is, in order for God's promise or grace to become our blessing—we must appropriate that promise or grace. For the Church to have God's presence, there is no other way.

The Church of the last days has the same misconception the Jews once had. The Jews assumed that since they had a covenant with God, and since they possessed the holy city Jerusalem, as well as the glorious holy temple, God's presence would be with them forever. They did not realize that there were conditions for God's presence, and therefore did not do according to God's commandments, statutes and ordinances; they did not practice righteousness according to God's law. How could they then expect God to carry out His covenant and fulfill His promise? As a result, the holy city was destroyed, the temple was burned, their homes were devastated, their kingdom was ruined, and they were dispersed all over the world until May 14, 1948, when their nation was reconstituted.

The Church today is indulging in the same kind of self-gratifying dream as well. She automatically assumes that since God has established her, God will naturally be with her forever. This is regardless of her holiness or her performance in fulfilling the required conditions for His presence. As a result, many ministries of the Church are comparable to those of the Israelites in Eli's time. The Israelites entered the battlefield, carrying the ark of the covenant that did not have God's presence. The sound of their shouting might have resounded throughout the earth, but the outcome was tragic—numerous soldiers and generals were killed, and the ark of the LORD was captured! In order for the Church to grow, we not only have to realize our need for God's presence, but we also have to diligently practice the conditions required for His presence.

Some may think that carrying out the required conditions to receive God's blessings is dependent on "works"—that is, on the Law; and that such dependence should not exist in the age of grace. They do not understand that the Holy Spirit never helps the lazy ones, nor do they realize that carrying out the conditions God requires is the only way leading to the enjoyment of God's grace. For instance, fresh air and sunlight are both gifts from God. If we desire to enjoy them, we must carry out the conditions to be in contact with them. Otherwise, fresh air and sunlight will forever exist to us only as objective realities, not subjective blessings.

2

DO ACCORDING TO GOD'S WORD

Moses was cognizant of the importance of having God's presence. When God announced that He would not go up with the Israelites to the promised land, Moses offered such a solemn prayer to God:

> If Thy presence does not go with us, do not lead us up from here....Is it not by Thy going with us, so that we, I and Thy people, may be distinguished from all the other people who are upon the face of the earth? (Ex. 33:15-16)

Can we then derive from his second prayer that the lack of distinction between the Church and the world is the result of God's absence from the Church?

Moses' successor, Joshua, also realized the paramount importance of having God's presence. Immediately after the death of Moses, he was blessed with this promise from God and was told of the required conditions. With faithfulness, the admirable Joshua fulfilled all the specified conditions and thus enjoyed all the blessings of this promise. God's presence empowered him to conquer thirty-one Canaanite kings; and thus the Israelites were able to establish a foothold in Canaan.

In the Bible, there are about 2,000 promises from God, most of which have conditions. The lazy nature of human flesh appreciates only the promises, not the conditions. In order to please man, some preachers totally exclude these conditions from their sermons on God's promises. Such preaching can be likened to a man drawing pictures of a cookie to satisfy hunger. As a consequence, people who listen can never obtain what has been promised, and will never be satisfied. Eventually, the highway leading to heaven is filled with spiritually starved souls.

Dear co-workers in Christ, when preaching on God's promises, please tell your congregation the conditions required for attaining them. Otherwise, you will deceive yourselves as well as others. May God have mercy upon us, that we will not be like the blind leading the blind.

The remainder of this chapter describes the four conditions required for God's presence. Each action verb introduces one condition:

- To do. . .
- To observe. . .
- To meditate. . .
- To trust. . .

To Do—"...so that you...do according to all that is written." (Josh. 1:8)

All Scripture is written for us to do accordingly. The Bible says,

> But prove yourselves doers of the word, and not merely hearers who delude themselves. (Jas. 1:22)

And, our Lord Jesus has also said,

> My mother and My brothers are these who hear the word of God and do it. (Luke 8:21)

Frequently preached from the pulpit in the last days is "what something is," but seldom "how something should be done." After the delivery of a beautifully outlined and presented sermon, the congregation often is still at a loss as to how God's truth should be applied to their daily lives.

Several years ago, I was invited to preach at the annual meeting of a certain denomination. There was a brief time for sharing before my message. One person, quoting Joshua 1:9 as the theme of his sharing, encouraged the congregation to trust in this promise—

> Do not tremble or be dismayed, for the LORD your God is with you wherever you go.

He seemed to have the gift of eloquence, and the congregation was beside itself with joy at the cadence of his voice. But, sitting in the last row, I almost shouted out, "Brother, you are lying! You are deceiving these honest souls with honey-coated words!" He told them what God's promise was, without even mentioning the conditions required (doing, observing, meditating and trusting in God's Word). How could they enjoy God's promise then? Following their discovery that they could not claim that promise, would they not doubt God's Word even more? Such impractical preaching is not only unprofitable, but also harmful!

How can we do according to God's Word then? We have to first observe His Word before we can do accordingly.

To Observe—"...that thou mayest observe ...all that is written...." (Josh. 1:8) [KJV]

This second condition is the primary reason why most Christians today cannot do according to God's Word. "To observe" in the Old Testament can be translated as "to keep," "to follow" and "to safeguard." Its other translations are "to preserve" (Mal. 2:7), "to guard" (Gen. 41:35), "to keep" (1 Sam. 9:24), "to keep for" (Ex. 22:7) and "to keep watch" (Ps. 141:3). In other words, the original meaning of "to observe" is "to keep or to safeguard God's Word in our heart."

"To observe" and "to do according to" often appear together in the Old Testament (ref.: Deut. 4:6; 5:1; 6:3; 7:11-12). Such usage is tantamount to saying that in order to do according to God's Word, we first have to observe His Word in our heart. The Bible tells us:

> For as he thinks within himself, so he is. (Prov. 23:7)

> For from it [the heart] flow the springs of life. (Prov. 4:23)

Even our Lord Jesus has said,

> The good man out of his good treasure brings forth what is good....(Matt. 12:35)

What a person's character is and how he behaves depend solely on his beliefs and conceptions. If God's Word is not in him, how can he do accordingly? When a person's mind is empty, how can his words and actions be rich in content? On the other hand, when a person is richly filled with God's Word, what he says and what he does will naturally be governed and administered by God's Word. Only then, can God's glory be manifested.

In order to do according to God's Word, we must first let His Word richly dwell in us; otherwise, all advice and encouragement are just wishful thinking, perceivable, but not attainable. How can we observe His Word in our heart then? To observe God's Word, we have to practice "meditation."

To Meditate—"This book of the law shall not depart from your mouth, but you shall meditate on it day and night...." (Josh. 1:8)

Meditation is a spiritual art and a form of worship. What a pity we Christians of the last days have forgotten all about this! No wonder our spiritual lives cannot grow.

Several years ago, I was invited to conduct a special series of seminars sponsored by a seminary. One day, after a meeting, a student approached me and asked if I had any secret in studying the Bible. My answer was, "No, I don't have any particular secret. Nevertheless, there is one thing I am afraid most seminarians today are unaware of—that is, the importance of meditation! Many a time, right after reading the Bible, we forget what we have just read. But, if we meditate on the passage for a couple of minutes after each reading to let God's Word dwell in us, then, over a period of time, we will be able to pool together various findings from previous meditations, and blend these findings together harmoniously. Gradually, we will have rich new insights in every verse of the Bible."

Some may think that meditation is a term used by other religions. This is true; other religions do meditate. Some universities even offer courses on meditation, teaching students to empty their minds of all thoughts, hoping that through such an action, they may have an "out of body" experience some day. This, of course, is very dangerous! Emptying one's mind will give place to evil spirits, and thus allow Satan opportunities to take advantage of the person. The meditation taught in our Bible, however, is none other than God's own revelation.

There are two words in the Old Testament that ought to be translated as "to meditate." Coincidentally, they are both found in Psalms 77:12 and 143:5.

> I will meditate on all Thy work,
> And muse on Thy deeds. (Ps. 77:12)
>
> I meditate on all Thy doings;
> I muse on the work of Thy hands. (Ps. 143:5)

Both verbs, "to meditate" and "to muse," should be translated as "to meditate." For instance, in Psalm 1, the one who yields his fruit in his season is the one who meditates on the law of the LORD day and night (vv. 2-3). And in Psalm 119, meditation can help us regard God's ways (v. 15), and handle those who talk against us (v. 23); but we need divine understanding from God in order to meditate (v. 27). The psalmist further says that he who knows how to meditate will have more insight than all his teachers (v. 99). Meditation is great!

I do suggest that if you spend half an hour on personal devotion each day, the best time allotment is 10 minutes in prayer, 10 minutes in Bible reading, and 10 minutes in meditation by asking questions with who, what, when, where, how and why. The initiation of something worthwhile is always difficult; perfection, however, is the product of constant practice. Meditation is no different.

To Trust—"Only be thou strong and very courageous,...observe to do according to all the law...." (Josh. 1:7) [KJV]

Before we can effectively "do according to," "observe" and "meditate" on God's Word, we need to have the prerequisite of trusting in His Word.

Most exegetical studies on Joshua 1:7 are influenced by its preceding verse, assuming that "be strong" and "courageous" refer to "not being afraid of the Canaanites" (v. 6). In reality, the subject of consideration in verse 7 is God's Word; and the verse demands that we have abundant faith in His Word. It is the same as Joshua's later encouragement to the leaders of the Israelites:

> Be very firm, then, to keep and do all that is written in the book of the law of Moses, so that you may not turn aside from it to the right hand or to the left.... (Josh. 23:6)

Many Christians of the last days are just like Gideon's 22,000 soldiers: timid, frightened, and with no faith in God's Word. They cannot meditate, and even if they try, their efforts are futile.

The conditions required for God's presence may be summed up as follows:

(1)   To have God's presence, we must do according to His Word;

(2)   To do according to His Word, we must let His Word dwell in us;

(3)   To let His Word dwell in us, we must know how to meditate;

(4)   To meditate, we must trust in His Word.

If we follow these four steps diligently, our God who is faithful will definitely be with us, as He has promised in the Great Commission, "and lo, I am with you always, even to the end of the age" (Matt. 28:20). Praise the Lord!

3

PASTORS MUST BE CALLED AND SENT BY GOD

Having an increase of 3,000 or 5,000 new believers in one single day was quite common during the Early Church Period. The cause for such a dramatic growth was not only the work of the Holy Spirit, but also the messages of the apostles. Unlike the false prophets in the Old Testament— whom God "did not send...or command," and who did not "furnish this people [the Israelites] the slightest benefit" (Jer. 23:32)—the apostles were sent by God and had the presence of God. The messages they preached pierced people's hearts, causing them to worship God and proclaim that God was truly among them (ref. 1 Cor. 14:25).

In recent years, I have had ample opportunity to preach to different Chinese churches at home as well as abroad. Through these occasions of involved contact and observation, the one conclusion that can be drawn for the stagnation in many churches is: Their pastors have yet to learn the art of preaching in a way that can satisfy the spiritual needs of their congregations.

Not too long ago, when I was preaching at a Chinese church on the East coast, the leaders of that church commented, "If our pastor can preach a sermon with substance only once every three months, we will be content!" Can a pastor who is incapable of such preaching and such feeding be called and sent by God? The answer, unfortunately, is obvious.

Years ago, a professor of Systematic Theology from a seminary on the West coast made this remark: "I think teaching and preaching are exactly the same!" I could not disagree more. Teaching and preaching belong to two totally different categories. As a seminary professor, he could not even differentiate between teaching and preaching. Can his students preach then? Again, the answer is a clear "No."

Standing at the pulpit, many seminary graduates of today can only give a lecture, but not preach a message. A pastor who does not know how to preach is likened to a chef who does not know how to cook! It is simply a fantasy to think that a restaurant with an unskilled chef will have a booming business.

A pastor has to be sent by God and be gifted in preaching before a church can have any growth. Otherwise, that pastor may need to consider another livelihood, so as to avoid deceiving himself, misleading others and, later, being judged by God.

A Pastor's Qualification

The qualification of a pastor, in fact, does not depend on whether he has a Master of Divinity degree or a Doctorate of Theology, nor does it matter whether he is trained as an apprentice or trained at a seminary. Rather, it is paramount that he has God's calling and gifts. The Bible says,

> How shall they preach unless they are sent?
> (Rom. 10:15)

The personnel for the kingdom of heaven are not volunteers (ref. Matt. 8:19), but an élite task force selected and called by God Himself! If on top of God's calling and gifts, a pastor also has seminarian training, then, of course, that would be superb. It would be like a beautiful peony being decorated with jade green leaves, each bringing out the beauty of the other.

The desolation in the Church of the last days is not due to the lack of pastors, but an abundance of pastors who serve without God's sending. Since they are not sent by God, how can they expect God to be responsible for them and provide them with His message? Not only is God not responsible, but He may also be against them (Jer. 23:30-31).

A Pastor's Foremost Task

The foremost task of a pastor is not visitation, but the distribution of spiritual nourishment to his congregation. It should be given at the proper time and according to their capacities, so as to sustain their spiritual needs. In addition to preaching on fifty-two Lord's days, there are other small meetings as well. A pastor therefore should have at least a hundred messages prepared each year for any contingency. If he does not have continuous provisions from God, the mere "canteen of water" collected from the seminary will soon run dry, and he will have no more messages to preach. His only choice is either repeating the same message again and again, or moving on to another church. Pastors who are truly sent by God should have an inexhaustible well of living water that they can draw from. Jeremiah has said, "They [God's lovingkindnesses and compassions] are new every morning" (Lam. 3:23). Praise the Lord!

Because of famous chefs and delicious food, many five-star restaurants in America are always packed, regardless of their remoteness. The same is true for a church. If a pastor receives his message from God every Lord's day, the sermon he preaches will make a significant difference. It will reveal the innermost secrets of the unbelievers so that, with humility, they will fall on their knees to worship God. It will also renew the minds of the believers so that gradually they will have the likeness of their Creator. Such a church will naturally grow, day by day.

Among all pastoral duties, the most difficult and most important task is to know, without doubt, the message God intends for him to preach each Lord's day. Sometimes, with God's blessing, the message may come on Monday, and then that week will be the most enjoyable week. But sometimes, even by Thursday, the message to be preached is still unclear. If the latter is the case, then the pastor should fast and pray fervently before God on Friday. Our spiritual awareness is often unblocked as soon as we start fasting and praying, and the message God intends will become crystal clear. This is speaking from my personal experience. Dear co-workers in Christ, please give it a try!

A Pastor's Remedy

To those pastors who are uncertain of God's calling, I sincerely suggest the following as a remedy. Our Lord Jesus said, "Therefore beseech the Lord of the harvest to send out workers..." (Matt. 9:38). This verse teaches us to pray to God if we want Him to send out workers.

The church I first pastored (in 1933) was a small one whose congregation constantly fought against one another. Following Sunday service each Lord's day, the two parties would pound on the table fighting and accusing one another as a matter of course. After pastoring them for half a year and seeing no improvement in sight, I started to doubt if I was called and sent by God. I began fasting and praying to God earnestly. One day, in a vision, I saw an angel summon me to an examination. After the examination, this angel told me, "You have passed. God has called you to preach to the world, that they may be convicted concerning sin, and righteousness, and judgment." From that moment onward, not only have my sermons been empowered by the Holy Spirit, touching those who listen, but God Himself has also been in charge of all situations, solving every problem that arises.

Our God is a faithful God! He remains faithful, for He cannot deny Himself. Dear co-workers in Christ, if you are uncertain of God's calling, please try fasting and praying to Him directly. He will answer you and guide your way according to His plan.

A Pastor's Deserved Honor

A pastor's own conviction of God's calling is of course essential to the growth of a church, but the congregation's love and prayer for their pastor are of equal significance. I often tell the brothers and sisters of my church, "If you don't pray for me, then, please don't blame me for not being able to preach a good sermon!"

In the past, pastors in mainland China were called "the gentlemen in-charge." To put it bluntly, the title meant "janitors." Pastors received no love, no respect and no encouragement from their congregation, but constant demands for harder work with little pay. The congregation seemed to be saying, "We want a fine horse that does not eat hay!"

A congregation that disrespects God's servant also disrespects God. How can they expect to have God's presence and have church growth when they are not reverent towards God? On the other hand, when a congregation and its pastor love one another and pray earnestly for one another, then the Almighty God Himself will certainly be with them. It is absolutely impossible for a church that has God's presence not to have growth.

4

CHRISTIANS MUST LOVE ONE ANOTHER

When the brothers and sisters of a church focus on putting themselves first, fighting for fame and grasping at benefits, and when they are unwilling to treat one another with sincerity, to act in one accord, and to have affinity for one another, God's presence will never be a reality among them. The Bible has stated,

No one has beheld God at any time; if we love one another, God abides in us.... (1 John 4:12)

The Early Church had God's presence not only because the apostles were called and sent by God, but also because the brethren loved one another.

It Is God's Commandment

God gave the Ten Commandments to the Israelites in the Old Testament, but He has given only one to the New Testament Christians. This commandment is:

> And this is His commandment, that we believe in the name of His Son Jesus Christ, and love one another, just as He has commanded us. (1 John 3:23)

On the surface, it seems that there are two commandments. In reality they are two aspects of one commandment, because the word "commandment" is singular in number in the original language. Its singularity has fully unfolded the significance of loving one another.

The common concept most Christians hold is, "Believing in our Lord Jesus is an absolute must, but loving one another is for our free will to choose." The Holy Spirit has, however, clearly pointed to a contrary concept: Loving one another and believing in our Lord Jesus are of equal importance. Believing in our Lord is an absolute must, and loving one another is also an absolute must. Since they are two aspects of one commandment, we cannot treat them with partiality. May the Church of the last days think thrice about this.

It Is Laying Down Oneself

"Loving one another" has been misunderstood and misinterpreted over and over again. The young people today, in particular, often confuse love with sex. This lustful animalism can in turn lead to evil ways. As a result, society is in chaos, families are breaking down, and man is acting like an animal. What then is "loving one another" after all? The Bible tells us:

> We know love by this, that He laid down His life for us; and we ought to lay down our lives for the brethren. (1 John 3:16)

The first half of this verse is easy to comprehend, because our Lord Himself demonstrated His love for us through death. But the meaning of the second half, "and we ought to lay down our lives for our brethren," is difficult to grasp. As we only have one life on this earth, does it mean that we can only love a brother once in this life? Such an explanation is certainly unacceptable! Therefore, let us go back to the original Greek language.

In the phrase "He laid down His life," originally "His life" is "His soul." This verse actually says,

29

> ...He laid down His soul for us; and we ought to lay down our souls for the brethren.

Since "soul" often means "self" in the Bible, then this verse can in fact be further interpreted as:

> We know love by this, that He laid down His self for us; and we ought to lay down ourselves for the brethren.

"To love" is to lay down one's "self"; and "to love one another" is brethren laying down their "selves" for one another. Any love that has a purpose or an intention which puts oneself first, is nothing but lust!

It Is Imitating The Lord

The soul consists of intellect, emotion and will. Since "to love" is to lay down one's soul, then "to love one another" can be characterized as below. For the sake of his brethren, a person is willing to lay down his **emotions** (his happiness, sorrow, love, hatred, desire and fear), his **intellect** (his opinions, goals, expectations and perceptions), and his **will** (his choices, rules and ideas).

Our Lord Jesus has set a good example for us. Because of His love for His parents, He laid down his desire for knowledge and returned to Nazareth with them. Because of His love for His disciples, He laid down his infinite understanding and put the disciples first in every matter. And, because of His compassion for the Canaanite woman, He laid down His rules and allowed her to share the crumbs that fell from the table.

In short, pure love does not include the least bit of "self." If a church can love one another in such a way, church growth will naturally "bloom abundantly and joy will be added to joy."

It Is Perfecting God's Love

The Bible says, "...if we love one another, God abides in us, and His love is perfected in us" (1 John 4:12). Loving one another is a condition necessary for God's presence as well as a means for perfecting His love.

The noun "love" is in the genitive case. A genitive case can be either objective or subjective; and in this verse, the latter is more appropriate. This love is God's love for us, because it is about the functions of loving one another—to have God's presence, and, to perfect His love.

What is the meaning of "His love is perfected"? All normal and pure love has three essential aspects: the object of love, the action of love, and the extension of love. We all know that God is love, but who is the object of God's love? He is Christ! Our gracious Lord has said this to God the Father, "...for Thou didst love Me before the foundation of the world" (John 17:24). It should be no surprise then, that a voice came out of the

31

heavens after His baptism, saying, "This is My beloved Son, in whom I am [was] well-pleased" (Matt. 3:17).

What is the action of God's love then? The Bible says,

> The Father loves the Son, and has given all things into His hand. (John 3:35)

> ...in His Son, whom He appointed heir of all things.... (Heb. 1:2)

This is the reason why God has created the whole universe: "...all things have been created by Him and for Him" (Col. 1:16).

To whom has God's love been extended? Our Lord Jesus has told His disciples that, "Just as the Father has loved Me, I have also loved you..." (John 15:9). Thanks be to our gracious Lord whose love for us is not a mere reflection of His sympathy, but an extension of the Father's love. How exciting and how joyous it is! Hallelujah!

Since one aspect of God's love is extension and we have enjoyed it through our Lord Jesus (ref. John 17:23), we should then extend it to brothers and sisters in Christ. Our Lord Jesus has said,

> This is My commandment, that you love one another, just as I have loved you. (John 15:12)

When God's children become lovers of self and are unwilling to love one another, they put a halt to the extension. As a consequence, the purpose of God's love cannot be achieved and thus cannot be perfected. May God help us to love one another, that His love will be perfected in us. When His love is nurtured in a church, the church will surely grow in Him.

It Is Through Practice

The apostles received this commandment of love directly from our Lord, and they later practiced it faithfully and continuously. As a result, "Behold, how loving Christians are towards one another!" became a remark of admiration and compliment from Gentiles towards Christians at that time. As for today, "loving one another" is only a slogan the Church chants mechanically, but cares little for. Its realization seems so distant that we do not know when it will come about. When a church does not understand the importance and essence of love, and does not practice its prerequisite of laying down oneself, it is impossible for God to be with her. May God have mercy upon us!

5

THE CHURCH MUST BE HOLY

In the Old Testament, God commanded the Israelites whom He had delivered from slavery to consecrate themselves and be a holy nation, so that His presence could be with them (Ex. 19:5, 6; Lev. 11:45). When the Israelites led a consecrated life, God responded in a loving manner, took care of them, and even dwelled among them. His presence was fully manifested as His glory filled the tabernacle and the holy temple at their dedications (Ex. 40:34-35; 1 Kin. 8:10, 11). On the other hand, when the Israelites refused to lead a consecrated life, or when the holy temple was filled with idols,

His presence departed from them (Ezek. 8:3, 5, 10, 14).

Although it was not God's desire to depart from the Israelites, His glory had no choice but to leave them in the end. His glory first went up from the cherub to the threshold of the holy temple (Ezek. 9:3) and stood over the threshold (Ezek. 10:4). From here it departed the threshold and stood over the cherubim (Ezek. 10:18). When the cherubim departed, it stood still at the entrance of the east gate of the holy temple (Ezek. 10:19), and then went up from the midst of the city to stand over Mount Olivet, which is east of the city. At last it went up and departed from the earth (Ezek. 11:22, 23).

The Israelites have lost God's presence since A.D. 70. Their houses were destroyed and their families were scattered; the whole nation became homeless, drifting from place to place. Had God not delivered them from such a miserable predicament, their nation would have met a tragic end a long time ago!

It is the same in the New Testament. At the onset of the Early Church Period, in order to sanctify the Church, God purged from within by bringing sudden death to Ananias and his wife for the lies they told. After that incident, the Bible says, "And all the more believers in the Lord, multitudes of men and women, were constantly added to their number" (Acts 5:14). As for Christians today, our Lord Jesus Christ Himself has become our sanctification (1 Cor. 1:30), but God still demands us to be holy in our daily living (1 Pet. 1:15). If the Church wants the reality of God's presence, she has to consecrate herself and be holy. God has repeatedly urged His people: "You shall be holy, for I am holy" (Lev. 11:44; 1 Pet. 1:16).

How can we consecrate ourselves and be holy then? First, we have to separate ourselves from ". . . unbelievers. . . lawlessness. . . darkness. . . Belial. . . idols. . . come out from their midst. . . and do not touch what is unclean. . ." (2 Cor. 6:14-17). Then, we have to perfect "holiness in the fear of God" (2 Cor. 7:1).

In the following pages, I have listed a few areas where we must consecrate ourselves in order to be holy, hoping that it will be useful to the Church of the last days.

Christians Must Be Holy (1 Cor. 6:11)

When the Israelites left Egypt, "a mixed multitude also went up with them" (Ex. 12:38). This mixed multitude caused the Israelites great sorrow and suffering in later days (Num. 11:4-5). Although their physical presence was in the desert, their hearts were still in Egypt—that is, their focus was on earthly things. Self-gratification became their god. From morning till night, they kept on yelling, "Give me! Give me!" They enjoyed luring the hearts of honest men with honeyed words. The adverse effects of their unholiness caused the Israelites to weep and Moses to beg for God to kill him. God was so angry that He wanted to wipe out the whole nation of Israel.

a. Less is better than more

In the early '70s, a young seminary graduate planned to start some pioneering work in a certain city. In preparation, he interviewed an elderly pastor, hoping to gain some insight from the pastor's extensive experiences. The elderly pastor kindly shared with him all the golden rules, such as—always being prepared, knowing the proper spiritual priorities, starting with the basics before proceeding to the profound, and setting examples by one's action. Before concluding his sharing, this veteran pastor solemnly warned him: Less is better than more! He also advised him not to overextend himself, nor set a foundation on the sand, lest he suffer bitterly later on. This young graduate responded with a smile and then left.

Later, it was said that he accepted everyone seeking church membership, regardless of their acceptance of Jesus as personal Savior. His attitude was "the more the better"! Three years later, as he aired his grievances to the same elderly pastor, he wept and begged for advice. Many in his congregation claimed to be Christians but had no eternal life; they fought for privileges but retreated from responsibilities. Such members were apt to mishandle church ministries. They truly were "always learning and never able to come to the knowledge of the truth" (2 Tim. 3:7). The elderly pastor said to him, "You've brought all these things upon yourself. Didn't I tell you three years ago 'less is better than more'? Didn't I warn you not to accept any member without first checking his spiritual life? You didn't listen. And now, you're suffering the consequences of your own doing." When a person brings disaster upon himself, he deserves it.

b. Beware of terminal diseases

The inability to distinguish the spiritual from the carnal, and the acceptance of all applications for church membership, have always been the mortal wound of the Chinese Church. They have already caused the Church to lose God's presence and the opportunities for church growth. If such a situation continues, the numerical increase is analogous to a temporary swollen face from self-inflicted slaps. We definitely cannot say that is healthy! Seats in every pew may be filled on Sunday, but the fact remains there are only a handful of people in prayer meeting, Bible study and Sunday school. How can they be so smug as to claim such an unnatural puffiness as church growth?

God's Church must be holy and glorious. But, when she is filled with people dead in trespasses and sins, as the holy temple was once filled with idols, what can our holy God do but depart from her? We Christians love the soul of every person on this earth, yet we should never allow anyone to hinder us from having God's presence, nor permit any person to destroy God's body. We love each and every cell of our body, yet we should never allow the existence of any cell that can poison or do harm to our body. We should always remove these harmful cells completely.

Unfortunately, people often allow cancerous cells to be injected into the Body of Christ. This is the reason why some churches today are suffering from terminal diseases!

c. Tidy the couch for guests

How can one be holy? Anyone who wants to be holy must first be in Jesus Christ, because He is our sanctification (1 Cor. 1:30). To be in Jesus Christ, we have to believe in His name; to believe in His name is to receive Him (John 1:12). What does it mean by "receiving Him" then? Let me borrow an idiom frequently employed in Chinese letter writing to clarify this point. In expressing one's welcome to friends and relatives coming for a visit, one often writes, "I tidy my couch to wait for your coming." "To tidy the couch" means to remove the dust from the couch; "to wait for" is to welcome with proper courtesy. Receiving (or believing in) Jesus is just as simple as that.

(1) Hand over to our Lord Jesus all the dirt and dust in our hearts, and disclose to Him all wickedness within us—this is "confession."

(2) Let the Lord bear all our iniquities to a "solitary land" (Lev. 16:22)—this is "forgiveness" and "deliverance."

(3) Invite the Lord into our heart as our Savior and King—this is "believing."

In other words, no man can be sanctified unless he believes in Jesus Christ! Only when a person willingly hands over his unrighteousness and unholiness to Jesus Christ, and only when he welcomes Him into his heart, can he then be sanctified.

God has told us, "Do not be bound together with unbelievers" (2 Cor. 6:14). Given this commandment, how can we expect God's presence in a church that is full of unbelievers? It is simply a daydreamer's fantasy if we insist on having church growth under such conditions.

Leaders Must Be Holy (Acts 20:28)

Not only should lay Christians be sanctified, but church leaders should also be holy. The failure of church leaders in conducting themselves as leaders and role models has been the primary cause for the stagnation of most Chinese churches in the past. Throughout the histories of Israel and Judah, God revealed to us that the fate of a country depended on the reigning king. When the king did right in the sight of God without deviation to evil ways, his populace would enjoy peace, harmony, happiness and prosperity, and his country would be strong and powerful. Otherwise, his country would either be raided and humiliated by neighboring countries, or infested by robbers and thieves! The importance of church leaders to a church is identical. It is no wonder that the Bible commands all church leaders:

> Be on guard for yourselves and for all the flock, ...to shepherd the church of God which He purchased with His own blood. (Acts 20:28)

a. The cause of the generation gap

Years ago, I often preached in the Mid-West. The brethren there told me about the seriousness of the generation gap in their churches, but I did not think much of it at first, until similar comments kept coming up repeatedly in other cities. Then, I began to do a study on this problem. The result of my study is this: The fundamental cause of a generation gap in a church is the elders' inability to conduct themselves as leaders, rather than the young people's prideful attitude!

Even though many church leaders may have the title "elder" or "deacon" printed on their business cards, yet they are titular elders and deacons, for they never act as nor serve as deacons or elders. Some will not come even to Sunday service unless the pastor invites them personally. How can they then expect their educated young people, who insist on striving for thoroughness in everything, to say "Amen" to them? Consequently, the two sides become as water and fire that cannot co-exist. All ideas and suggestions from the elderly, no matter right or wrong, will naturally be rejected by the young people. Fighting and quarreling at business meetings become a common practice. New believers shake their heads and sigh; some even stumble. How pitiful it is!

Therefore, church leaders who are "lovers of self, lovers of money. . .unholy. . .unloving, irreconcilable, malicious gossips. . .brutal. . .reckless, conceited. . .rather than lovers of God". (2 Tim. 3:1-5) should resign from their positions. Their resignation would be a gesture to show their self-reproach. Only then may they avoid becoming a stumbling block to others, and thus escape God's judgments later (Matt. 18:6).

b. The possible solution

"If such a generation gap has been deeply rooted in the church for a long time, what should we do then?" My answer to this question is, "With men this is impossible, but with God all things are possible" (Matt. 19:26)!

Several years ago, I was invited to preach in a church in Southern California. In that church, there was a leader who did not really know the Lord yet and was, therefore, ignorant of spiritual matters. He intentionally acted against the young pastor of the church by repeatedly forcing the pastor into some very embarrassing situations. The young pastor sought my counsel and I shared with him, "There is only one solution—prayer! You should ask God to either change him or send him away. God will definitely open a door for you." This young pastor took the advice; he fasted and prayed diligently regarding the matter. Shortly thereafter, that elder did not come anymore. Co-workers who love our Lord Jesus, you can try to handle similar problems in the same way too!

c. The neglected principles

A church must have these four essential principles as their crucial pillars of support: knowledge, faith, behavior and discipline. A church is likened to a building. Lacking any one of these principles will cause a slant or even a collapse of the whole church. While the church must have all four principles, they must also give each of them **equal** emphasis.

If "knowledge" is unduly emphasized, we will easily repeat the mistakes of the Pharisees, pridefully assuming ourselves as "a guide to the blind, [and] a light to those who are in darkness" (Rom. 2:19). In reality, what we have secured so far is just some unproven knowledge. What good can that kind of knowledge be?

If "faith" is unduly emphasized, we will easily become emotional maniacs. When we conclude that everything in Christ is merely an activity of the emotions, our concentration, of course, will be centered solely on the enjoyment of our sentiments, instead of the cultivation of truth and spiritual edification.

If "behavior" is unduly emphasized, we will think that all achievements depend on our own efforts. Then, what difference is there between our faith and those of other religions?

If we have the above three but lack "discipline," we are like a man who plants a vineyard without putting a fence around it. Wild beasts can enter, trampling the vineyard at their pleasure. The harvest of the grapes is out of the question, and the destruction of the vineyard is certain.

Therefore, a church has to heed not only the first three principles, but especially the fourth one. Negligence and lack of application of the fourth principle leads to the fruitlessness of many churches today.

d. The leaders' pledge

All deacon candidates of the First Chinese Baptist Church of Los Angeles have to pledge faithfulness to God, to the Church and to their offices. Here is their pledge for your reference.

"Ten 'MUSTS' For A Deacon Candidate In The Church"

(1)　Must have the desire to serve the Lord as a deacon and the willingness to honor one another.

(2)　Must pursue the requirements set forth in 1 Tim. 3:1-10.

(3)　Must study the Bible and pray every day and give tithes cheerfully and regularly.

(4)   Must be married and the wife must be willing to assist her husband as a deacon to the best of her ability.

(5)   Must be able to teach Sunday school.

(6)   Must be willing to serve the Lord in any capacity, especially in visitation.

(7)   Must attend all the basic meetings, such as worship services, Sunday school, prayer meetings, officers' meetings and business meetings; and support all Church organizations and projects.

(8)   Must participate in training opportunities and the training of others through the Church Training Program or other programs.

(9)   Must set a good example before younger Christians. Never argue with them or get angry with them without a training purpose.

(10)   Must work with the pastors.

Finances Must Be Sanctified (Prov. 15:8, 21:27; 1 Tim. 6:9-10)

While Dwight L. Moody was ministering in Chicago, he spoke on "The Path to Wealth." There were three main points to his sermon. During his sharing on the first point, "exert yourself diligently to earning money," loud applause from the congregation resounded through the giant hall. When he talked about the second point, "exert yourself industriously to saving money," again, loud applause rang through the hall. But, as soon as he came to the third point, "exert yourself zealously to offering money," the whole congregation was quiet, so quiet that even a pin drop could be heard!

This incident merely elucidates the reason why many churches often cannot make ends meet. Nowadays, Christians who are willing to demonstrate their love for God through money are indeed scarce.

Aside from stinginess towards God, we have to take precautions on other money-related matters as well. Failure to heed these precautions will cause God's absence in our church, and our financial situation will deteriorate even further!

a. Don't follow the vicious cycle

It is true that a hungry man cannot be too choosy of his food. Likewise, due to financial pressure, some churches are apathetic towards right and wrong. Their attitude of "the more money the better," and their disregard for the intention of the giver or the source of the money, have opened a gate for unrighteous, dirty money to sneak into the holy treasury of God's Church. God has commanded us, "You shall be holy for I am holy" (1 Pet. 1:16). When a church's treasury is defiled, how can the church expect our holy God to be with her?

The Old Testament records that God's glory (which is God's presence) departed from the Israelites when His holy temple was filled with idols (Ezek. 8). And the New Testament explains that a "...covetous man...is an idolator..." (Eph. 5:5). When a church's treasury is defiled, the church is not only covetous (which is equivalent to idolatrous), but also covetous of unrighteous money. What can God do but depart from her?

Then, the vicious cycle begins. Without God's presence, the apathetic church will surely face financial difficulties. The more difficult her financial situation, the more ways her leaders will try to raise funds. The more they try to raise funds, the more they fall into the trap of being unrighteous. The more unrighteous they become, the greater the possibility of God departing from them. This kind of cause and effect relationship often drives a church into a hopeless situation.

b. Don't confuse right and wrong

"A man of virtue loves money, but gets it in the right way." This is an ancient Chinese teaching. Some churches of the last days basically are not concerned about whether it is "the right way" or "the wrong way" as long as there is a way to obtain money. (Some missionary organizations are so depraved that they use piety as a means for material gain. Brothers and sisters who love our Lord should be aware of this.) When a holy organization degenerates to such a depravity, how can it expect to have the presence of our God?

A church in a big city in North America was experiencing some financial difficulties due to their church building project. In order to raise funds, they organized the congregation into small groups to solicit donations door to door in Chinatown. The brothers and sisters of that church, therefore, went knocking on doors for money. As soon as the door of a certain family was opened, they could clearly see that people inside were in the heat of gambling. After the gamblers realized the reason for their visit, one gambler picked up a five dollar bill from the gambling table and threw it to them. These brothers and sisters accepted the bill, said "thank you" and left! Since they used such dirty money to build God's holy temple, how could they expect God's presence to be with them? Immediately following the completion of the building, the church split apart. The pastor left with a group of brothers and sisters, leaving the rest of the congregation dumb-founded. It was such an irony to the whole church building project.

After Judas "threw...into the sanctuary" the thirty pieces of silver which he obtained from betraying Jesus, the chief priests picked up all thirty pieces of silver and said, "It is not lawful to put them into the temple treasury, since it is the price of blood" (Matt. 27:5-6). Even these priests and Pharisees who used piety as a means for material gain, could distinguish the sacrilegious from the holy. The Church of the last days, however, purposely ignores the distinction between right and wrong, and thus knowingly permits unrighteous money to defile the holiness of God. It comes as no surprise, then, that God's presence will depart from her (Ref. Ezek. 8-10).

c. Don't fantasize

The Bible says, "The sacrifice of the wicked is an abomination to the LORD" (Prov. 15:8), and "The sacrifice of the wicked is an abomination, / How much more when he brings it with evil intent!" (Prov. 21:27).

Who are the "wicked" ones? According to the definition in the Bible, they are not the unforgivable, heinous criminals, but "those who forget God" (Ps. 9:17; 50:16, 18). To God they are abominable and wicked because they forget God— they forget His love, His righteousness, and His holiness! It is true that they bring forth their offerings to God, yet there is no fear of God in their heart, but evil intent.

What does "evil intent" mean? "Evil intent" is an intention to bribe God and to defraud one's own conscience. For instance, a man who has knowingly accepted some unrighteous money, is bothered by his own conscience afterwards. Although no one else has any knowledge of his evil deed, yet it is clear to him that God knows about it and his own conscience knows about it as well. This deed keeps coming up in his thoughts in the quiet of the night. Burdened with guilt and shame, and overwhelmed with feelings of unworthiness, he still does not want to, nor dare to, face the reality. Instead, he fantasizes that, perhaps, with a large contribution to a church, God may be pleased (or should we say "bribed"), and therefore disregard his evil deed.

Alas, this man does not know that Jehovah God is the One who

> . . .will by no means leave the guilty unpunished, visiting the iniquity of fathers on the children and on the grandchildren to the third and fourth generations. (Ex. 34:7)

Our God is willing to "sympathize with our weaknesses" (Heb. 4:15), but He will never make any concession to our sins! He has clearly warned us, "Truly I say to you, you shall not come out of there, until you have paid up the last cent" (Matt. 5:26). Because of His righteousness, He has prepared for us the sin offering through the blood of our Lord Jesus Christ. God does not want our bribe, but desires our confession of sins! He has promised us, "If we confess our sins, He is faithful and righteous to forgive us our sins and to cleanse us from all unrighteousness" (1 John 1:9). Praise the Lord!

d. Don't be greedy

The Chinese in North America often describe Christians as lazy and greedy! The first description that Christians are lazy is a pure conjecture out of ignorance. In order to satisfy the desire, or the necessity, of earning more money, most first-generation Chinese immigrants often work with extreme diligence from dawn to midnight without any break. When they observe their Chinese Christian acquaintances going to church so frequently, they immediately conclude that attending church is just an excuse to avoid working hard. Therefore, Christians are lazy. This observation, of course, is uncalled for.

As for the second description that Christians are greedy, there is a good reason for this. Many Chinese churches are uninformed concerning the cultivation of love for God, but they are experts when it comes to squeezing money from their congregations. Some pastors will ask for monetary donations as soon as they are at the pulpit; basically there is no other sermon aside from this topic. One Lord's day, a Christian came to worship with us. When asked why she did not go back to her own church, she replied, "Whenever our pastor preaches, he asks for donations. It bores me to death!" Since some churches have such an insatiable covetousness towards God's holy offering, how can unbelievers not draw the conclusion that Christians are greedy?

As a remedy to such a bad reputation, one church in North America determined not to accept offerings from unbelievers. Of course, there were leaders who did not agree to this decision in the beginning, thinking that when people had the willingness to offer to God, it must be good.

Nevertheless, after a careful study on the warnings in the book of Proverbs, they not only refused to accept any unrighteous money, but also announced clearly before the collection of offerings, that unbelievers were not to participate in the worship with offerings. The total offering in that church is now over twenty-five thousand dollars each Lord's day! We can truly say that with God's presence, everything is blessed.

In short, "the love of money is a root of all sorts of evil" (1 Tim. 6:10)! This warning is not only for individuals but also for the Church as well. If a church does not heed this warning, but longs for money and defiles her finances, not only will she subsequently lose God's presence, but she will also wander away from the faith as well as pierce her pastors, elders, deacons and congregation with many a pang of guilt (1 Tim. 6:10).

6

BE A TRAINING CENTER

What is a church? Some say that a church is the place where we worship God on the Lord's day; or where we listen to a pastor preach for the perfection of our spirituality; or where Christians fellowship with one another and serve God together. These, however, are merely the functions of a church. As for the essence of a church, we have yet to define it! Based on the meaning of the Greek word for "church," some say that a church is a group of people who "have been called out" from the world by God. And some even quote from the epistles and say that a church is "the household of God," and "the pillar and support of the truth" (1

Tim. 3:15). These statements only further explain the origin, the fellowship and the principle of a church; but as for her commission and ministries, elucidation is still lacking! In other words, the true meaning of "a church" remains an intricate puzzle to many Christians today.

In our Lord's references to the Church in Matthew Chapters 16 and 18, He only talked about her name, her foundation, her authority, and her victory in Him, but did not reveal in detail her commission or her ministries. This was always a big mystery to me in the past. For a truth as important as the doctrine of the Church, the Head of the Church, our Lord Jesus Christ, has surprisingly left us with no revelation regarding her commission and her ministries! It was not until one day when I studied the Lord's Great Commission in Matthew Chapter 28, that I suddenly came to the realization that—the great revelation of the Church is in our Lord's Great Commission!

This Great Commission is also the most important condition required for God's presence. May our gracious Father open our eyes to fully comprehend its meaning.

Most Christians think that the verb "Go" is the word of paramount importance in the Great Commission. Since the verb "Go" is translated as the imperative mood in the English Bible, we naturally assume that "to evangelize the world" is the theme of the Great Commission. Such an interpretation has put the shoe on the wrong foot. No Christian can dispute the fact that "to evangelize the world" is one of the main tasks delegated to the Church by our Lord Jesus Christ. The sole importance of this task, however, is not the theme of the Great Commission!

There are four verbs in the Great Commission: "go," "make disciples," "baptize" and "teach." Only the verb "make disciples" is in the imperative mood; all the other three are participles or verbal adjectives. Therefore, the precise translation should be:

> **Going** therefore, you **must make disciples** of all the nations, **baptizing** them in the name of the Father and the Son and the Holy Spirit, **teaching** them to observe all that I commanded you; and lo, I am with you always, even to the end of the age.

In other words, "go" is not a command, but "make disciples" is, and it is also the main theme of the Great Commission.

In light of this, a church is none other than a **school** that enrolls students of Christ from all the nations, a **training center** for the personnel of God's kingdom, and a **seminary** of divine doctrines. Since a church is a school, it needs good students; in order to have good students the following steps are essential:

- Recruiting
- Registering
- Teaching

Recruiting: "Go Therefore...." (Matt. 28:19)

We often hear pastors making intense appeals from the pulpit to brothers and sisters sitting comfortably in the pews to go and share the gospel. The usual response from the congregation is: "You go and spread the gospel! Since you're a seminary graduate, you should know the Bible very well. As for us, we don't even understand the Bible, let alone know how to share it!" This is a sad reality. No matter how exhausted these anxious pastors are, nor how hoarse their voices may become, those brothers and sisters sitting in the pews are not only indifferent, but they have also hardened their hearts.

Our Lord Jesus never asked us to preach theology to the unbelievers, nor to teach them the Bible. On the other hand, He did tell us to witness to them, as He once said, "You are witnesses of these things" (Luke 24:48). You may wonder what witnessing is. To witness is to simply tell what you have experienced. What do we give witness to, then? We give witness to the "repentance for forgiveness of sins" (Luke 24:47-48).

If you have truly received Jesus as your personal Savior, you should have a born-again experience. Your order of priorities, pattern of thinking and value system should be different after becoming a Christian. Grab hold of every opportunity to share with others these three aspects of your personal experience: your situation before salvation; your experience in receiving Jesus as your personal Savior; and the blessings you received after salvation. The Holy Spirit can work in the listeners' hearts and help them realize that God will save them, just as He has saved you!

There is one important aspect you have to remember though, otherwise all your efforts may be in vain. After your testimony, remember to ask him, "Sir, are you willing to receive Jesus as your personal Savior just as I did?" The response may surprise you, "I am willing!" Then, you should lead him before our Lord Jesus by praying together with him—pray one sentence and ask him to repeat it after you; help him to confess his sins and invite Jesus into his heart. After the prayer, ask him, "Can you tell me where Jesus is now?" Amazingly, eight or nine out of ten people will point to their heart and say, "Jesus is here!" Blessed brothers and sisters, we should take advantage of the opportunity we still have to witness for our Lord, lest we meet our gracious Lord empty-handed.

What should we do, if someone is unwilling to receive the Lord right away? We should never force anyone to receive the Lord, but provide him with a remedy for future use. Ask him if he can do you a favor. Most likely he will say, "Okay, if I can. What's that?" Your answer should be, "Of course you can! Please pray this prayer for yourself everyday: 'God, I am willing to believe in you, but I don't know how. Please show me!'" If he is willing to make this promise and fervently prays that prayer, sooner or later he will meet God and become a Christian. Some need to pray for three or four days; some, ten or more. Some may even meet

God on that same day! When a person opens his heart to God, our God who is faithful will certainly enter in. He will never be late. Hallelujah! Even if that person does not keep his promise to pray for himself daily, there is no need for disappointment. How do you know he will not recall your testimony some time in the future and receive the Lord then?

Registering: "...baptizing them in the name of the Father and the Son and the Holy Spirit...." (Matt. 28:19)

Following a successful campaign of recruitment, many students will apply for admission. At that time, the Admissions Office of the school will carefully examine each application, transcripts, recommendation letters, and so on, to determine whether admission should be granted. Only those who are qualified will be allowed to register. Suppose there is a certain school that admits students based on their ability to pay tuition rather than their academic achievements, and after admission, gives students no guidance to their academic studies or their preparation for a future career. Society does have a name for such a school: "phony"! It is embarrassing to say that quite a few churches today are phony. How can these churches have a future?

If a church wants to have a bright and successful future, her standards for the acceptance of new members ought to be very strict. Before baptizing or accepting a person as part of the Body of Christ, the church should first investigate thoroughly the following. Has he been truly born again? Have his priorities, thoughts and values been changed? Does he rely on God through prayer in his daily life? Does he trust in God's Word in his Christian walk? Negligence of a thorough investigation will put us in the same category as the Scribes and the Pharisees of Jesus' time, who traveled about on sea and land to make one proselyte. When a proselyte was made, they made him a "son of hell" (Ref. Matt. 23:15).

Perhaps some may argue, "Didn't our Lord Jesus tell us, 'Allow the tares to grow together with the wheat until harvest'?" Such an interpretation is a result of inaccurate study of the Bible. Thanks be to our Lord who has explained this parable to us in detail. "The field" is "the world," not "the Church" (Matt. 13:38). The world may have a mixture of good and bad, but the Church should only be an organization of the citizens of heaven. If any brother in the Church leads an unruly life, not according to the Bible, we should keep aloof from him (2 Thess. 3:6); or not associate with him; or even as the Bible says, remove him from among ourselves (1 Cor. 5:11-13). It is a lie to claim that you desire good health, prosperity and a bright future for your flock while you allow foxes and wolves to run around freely in the fold!

Teaching: "teaching them to observe all that I commanded you...." (Matt. 28:20)

After registration, classes begin. Teaching is not only a moral obligation of the school, but also a matter of course. Unfortunately, many churches pay little attention to the importance of teaching. Some have newcomer classes or Bible study groups for new Christians, so as to help them establish a solid foundation for the understanding of the Bible, as well as the development of spiritual life. This great task of training is considered to have been completed once these new Christians are baptized. After baptism, they are left on their own without further discipleship or guidance towards spiritual growth. Some churches even hold the unhealthy concept that further training of Christians is basically insignificant as long as they are saved. As a result, the shortage of personnel has become the mortal wound of many churches for generations!

A careful study of the Bible will reveal how God considers the teaching ministry of paramount importance. In the Old Testament, God not only repeatedly commanded the Levites to teach the Israelites (Deut. 11:19; 33:10), but also chose Abraham to be the Father of His holy nation, that Abraham might command his children and his household after him, to keep the way of God (Gen. 18:19). King David asked God to forgive his sins so that he could "teach transgressors Thy [His] ways, / And sinners will be converted to Thee [God]" (Ps. 51:13). The revival in the middle of King

Jehoshaphat's reign took shape because of the teaching by the Levites (2 Chr. 17:9).

It is the same in the New Testament. The church in Jerusalem was blessed because they "were continually devoting themselves to the apostles' teaching" (Acts 2:42). Not only was Paul a teacher of the Gentiles himself (1 Tim. 2:7), but he also charged Timothy to teach "faithful men, who will be able to teach others also" (2 Tim. 2:2). Our Lord Jesus, the one who had "come from God as a teacher" (John 3:2), repeatedly emphasized the importance of teaching in His ministry. His method of evangelism was first to enlighten the audience through His teaching, and then to draw them towards God through His preaching (Matt. 9:35; 11:1). He applied this method to both the Samaritan woman (John 4) and the man blind from birth (John 9). His promise to us is this: Whoever keeps the commandments of God and teaches them to others, will not only have a part in "the kingdom of heaven" but also "shall be called great in the kingdom of heaven"(Matt. 5:19). No wonder one of the qualifications the Bible requires of God's servants is to be "able to teach others" (2 Tim. 2:2, 24). Thus, great is the office and responsibility of a Sunday school teacher!

Many churches cannot grow because they do not realize the importance of Sunday school. Their indifference to this aspect of church growth is rooted in their ignorance of the true essence of a church. If they knew that a church is a school of God, then they would immediately realize that among all activities in a church, besides Sunday worship, none can be more important and more appropriate than Sunday school. Experience tells us that what the congregation can remember from a Sunday sermon is just a sketchy outline. To really taste God's Word in depth, the congregation has to depend on Sunday school.

In 1976, I spoke at a conference sponsored by the Chinese Coordination Center of World Evangelism in Hong Kong. Some conferees shared with me that their pastor not only neglected their Sunday school, but also arrogantly made numerous excuses, preventing those who had a burden for this ministry from seeking his guidance. In this case, the congregation wanted to grow, but the pastor deterred it. This is truly incomprehensible!

The Church of the last days has gravely underestimated the importance of this ministry, while other world religions, such as Buddhism, have unexpectedly placed teaching as their very first priority. They have made determined efforts, disregarding failures and obstructions, to imitate Christian churches and their imitations are comparable. They have Sunday school similar to ours every Sunday, and Vacation Bible School similar to ours every summer. No wonder Buddhist churches are prosperous and are continuously multiplying. Upon reading such reports, the pitiful picture of many Christian churches comes to my mind, and their wickedness and laziness saddens my heart.

In recent years, when preaching at different churches, the writer has frequently been asked the secret of managing a good Sunday school. His answer has always been the same—"In order to have a good Sunday school, we must have good Sunday school teachers!" The expression, "Having the right man can accomplish many things," is an ancient teaching of the Chinese, and the principle by which God works. When God had Noah, then the ark was made; when there was Moses, then the exodus came; when Paul appeared, then the Gentile Church was established. In the same manner, when the church has good Sunday school teachers, then there will be a good Sunday school; and when there is a good Sunday school, there will be church growth. Many churches consider Sunday school a nursery in disguise or a dispensable decoration. No wonder little attention is directed to the quality of Sunday school teachers. As a result, most Sunday school ministries harbor no ambition for achievement and are merely struggling for existence.

The fact that good Sunday school teachers are a must for a good Sunday school needs no further deliberation. But how can we have good Sunday school teachers? Below are some suggestions from personal experience.

a. Be a "little" pastor—your class is a "little" church

The position of a Sunday school teacher in a church is exalted and glorious—a "little" pastor of the class. Every teacher should therefore exert himself always to be a good shepherd, that he may be counted as worthy of God's calling. As a good shepherd, he should at least do the following:

(1)   Try his very best to bring his unsaved students around to the acceptance of Jesus Christ as their personal Savior;

(2)   Edify and equip his students in every aspect that they may enjoy an abundant life in Christ;

(3)   Visit or telephone the ones who are absent to express sincere concern;

(4)   Pray for his students regularly;

(5)   Comfort those who are in sorrow;

(6)   Encourage those students who are disheartened.

In short, a Sunday school teacher is the pastor of his class of ten or fifteen students (like a small church). All these years, Chinese churches have been like scattered sand, without much sound organization. If Sunday school teachers consider their pastor to be the president of a country and themselves to be governors under the president, and if they respect one another through their show of cooperation, then their church will have not only an organizational system, but will also possess a very good cell structure. The potential for church growth will then become very promising.

b. Be a creative artist—the lesson is a personification of the Sunday school teacher

The difference between general education and Sunday school is comparable to that between Western cookery and the Chinese culinary art. The former is scientific: How much each ingredient should be, how long the whole mixture should be baked or cooked, and how hot the oven or the stove should be. The latter is artistic. A Chinese cook never follows any recipe. Through experience and occasional tasting while cooking, a cook can freely alter the ingredients and their quantities, the length of cooking, as well as the temperature required. The end result—the four dishes and one soup—is always complete with color, aroma and flavor. That sweet aroma remains for a long, long time!

A Sunday school teacher should consider himself an artist if he desires an effective ministry. A work of art is the personification of the artist; and, the presentation of a lesson is also the personification of the Sunday school teacher—the whole lesson is an effusion of the teacher's life. Only in this way, then, can the students enjoy the lesson and be blessed. They will surely attend the class every Lord's day, and they may bring their friends and relatives as well. Church growth will eventually come about. Therefore, Sunday school teachers should first pay close attention to themselves and then to their own teaching (ref. 1 Tim. 4:16). Our Lord Jesus has said, "A good tree cannot produce bad fruit, nor can a bad tree produce good fruit" (Matt. 7:18).

c. Be a faithful and sensible steward—teach according to the needs of your students

A grocery store is complete with various kinds of baby food, but no wise mother will purchase a large quantity just because of the bountiful stock, good quality or good bargains, without first finding out her baby's needs. Nor will she force feed her baby, causing him/her indigestion or other harm, without paying attention to the feeding schedule and the quantity her baby can consume. A wise mother will only purchase what is rich in nutrition and appropriate for her baby, and then feed that baby according to its schedule and capacity.

Sunday school teachers should also feed their students in the same manner, according to their pace and capacity. Never try to "force the whole Bible down their throats," solely because it is God's Word. All Scripture is good, but teaching according to each student's need is also an obvious principle in the Bible. In short, as long as the students are well fed and have healthy digestion, church growth will not be far away.

d. Be a painstaking laborer—nothing is ever worthwhile without hard work

Stemming from insufficient spiritual experience and the absence of formal training, many Sunday school teachers often just ramble on and on unintelligibly in class. Their spiritual life and their basic teaching techniques reveal their misconception about the value of Sunday school. They do not even know the following basics concerning the preparation for a lesson:

- How to create a vivid introduction—with a good introduction, the lesson is already half there;

- How to systematically present the lesson—incongruous explanations and explications will only arouse apathy;

- How to help students appropriate or apply the truth—that God's Word will not be in vain;

- How to conclude the lesson—that it becomes a must for the students so that they will do according to God's Word.

Teachers often apply the method of teaching literature, or the techniques of teaching chemistry to the teaching of God's Word. As a result, God's living Word of the Truth is taught as the letter of the Law that kills (2 Cor. 3:6).

Students are very smart. When a teacher is impious in his prayer life, or unfaithful in his preparation for the lesson, or insincere in his teaching, students can sense it intuitively. Over a period of time, they distrust and lose respect for that teacher. The lurking dangers can be anticipated. In short, the outward appearance is a reflection of the inner self. If a Sunday school teacher does not enrich himself through painstaking preparation, but continues to teach despite the absence of spiritual nourishment for his students, the disastrous effects will certainly be grave. The following suggestions will be helpful to the preparation for lessons:

(1)   Have your students in mind:

        (a) Understand their background, spirituality, characteristics, peculiarities, and so on, that you may teach according to their ability and need.

        (b) Pray for each student by name, and pray for their families.

        (c) Recall their reactions to your last lesson.

(2)   Have the lesson in mind:

(a) Study the passage thoroughly until its main theme is clear to you.

(b) Based on the main theme from your study, construct a complete outline (The material in the teacher's quarterly often cannot meet the needs of a local church. For effectiveness, Sunday school teachers should develop their own curriculum).

(c) Examine the content of the outline carefully: Is the explanation of the passage clear? Is the application of truth practical? Has the motivation for application been suggested?

e.   *Be a wise teacher—ask God for wisdom*

Spiritual knowledge and wisdom have their respective domains. The former is the knowledge of God's truth. The latter is the skillful application and administration of the revealed knowledge, that a particular truth may be clearly demonstrated, and its purpose (God's desire) may be achieved. For instance, in the parable of the ten virgins, they all had the knowledge of how the oil should be used, but only five of them had the wisdom to administer and apply the oil to achieve its purpose. Sunday school teachers should have both the knowledge and the wisdom in teaching and in winning souls, as the Bible says, "he who is wise wins souls" (Prov. 11:30).

A Sunday school is not only the education department of a church, but also a fishing boat that draws up souls; otherwise, it contributes nothing to the growth of a church. The wisdom that wins souls is certainly not "the wisdom of this world" but "all that God has prepared for those who love Him" (1 Cor. 2:9). All that God has prepared for us (or God's grace), is objective. In order for the objective promise to become our subjective reality or experience, we have to appropriate that promise. This is an important spiritual principle! James has rightly said, "If any of you lacks wisdom, let him ask of God...and it will be given to him" (Jas. 1:5).

Sunday school teachers should therefore appropriate this wisdom God has promised them, through supplications day and night. The Holy Spirit will certainly bestow upon them this utterance of wisdom as it is promised. Their teaching may then be clear and dynamic with rich insights from every verse of the Bible, just as the "head of a household, who brings forth out of his treasure things new and old" (Matt. 13:52). With such splendid and rich teachings, unsaved students may receive the Lord Jesus as their personal Savior, and thus become children of God. Those who have already believed may march forward in God's truth to maturity in Christ.

f. Be a worker of faith—not by might nor by power, but by the Spirit of God

Both the initiation and the termination of a spiritual ministry are in God's command. Sunday school teachers should assure themselves that they are working together with God (not that God works for them, but they work for God). God, who is the head of the Sunday school, will never forsake us, but guide and help us in every way. Without His presence, all efforts spent in the preparation of Sunday school lessons, no matter how thorough and how painstaking, are nothing but striving after the wind. Therefore, Sunday school teachers should have this faith: We are teaching in the name of the Lord and He is in our midst (Matt. 18:20). For the sake of His kingdom, our Lord who is faithful, will certainly be working with us.

According to statistics, the percentage of people over 40 years old who receive Christ is extremely small, especially among the Chinese. The reasons for such a low percentage among this generation of Chinese are two-fold: their extreme superstition towards idols (money, in particular) and the bad impressions from past experiences with the Church. Without a complete removal of their prejudice, and a correction of their misconceptions, it is almost impossible for this group to receive Christ. The removal of prejudice should start with their children who have never harbored such ill feelings towards God's Church, and therefore are more apt to receive the Lord. When they realize that all the wonderful changes in the lives of their children are due to the acceptance of Christ, they will definitely have deep appreciation and desire for that grace which their children enjoy (and which they lack). There was a devout youth who loved the Lord deeply. One day, both of his parents suddenly asked him, "Can we go to Sunday service with you?" As soon as they came, they received Christ and joined the church soon afterwards.

g. Be an expert in outline construction—speak with logic and truth

A shortage of Sunday school teachers in a newly established church is a normal phenomenon. The only alternative is the recruitment and training of those available in that church. In fact, if a pastor has the gift and wisdom of training teachers, even a grade school graduate can become an excellent teacher. However, most churches today are in such an urgent need for Sunday school teachers, that basically it is impossible to wait for the candidates' completion of regular formal training. Therefore, I cautiously propose a fast-track method as the solution— training teachers with the method of outline construction for Sunday school lessons. If a teacher comprehends the theme and content of the lesson, he will be very confident of what he should teach and emphasize. Such teaching will never be in a total disarray or without substance! With caution, I propose the "Ten MUSTS" for the construction of a lesson outline.

"Ten 'MUSTS' For The Construction Of A Lesson Outline":

(1)   First examine yourself carefully. See if there is anything that may impede the illumination and guidance of the Holy Spirit.

(2)   Have a deep conviction that the Spirit of Truth will lead you into Truth.

(3)   Pray earnestly, study the Bible carefully—examine the text to define the main theme of the passage.

(4)   Based on the background, the age and the spiritual needs of your students, select an appropriate topic for the lesson.

(5)   Use the "who, what, where, when, why, and how" to reflect on the passage and construct the outline.

(6)   Outline the passage according to the order of the verses as closely as possible.

(7)   The main theme must be consistent throughout the outline, but do not distort the passage.

(8)   Understand the characteristics of the outline: didactic, exhortative, corrective or consolatory, so as to avoid any inconsistency in the tone of voice and attitude when you teach.

(9)   Use parallel words or syntactical forms in the outline if possible, that your students may better recall the lesson.

(10)   Examine carefully to see if the explanation, application and motivation are sufficient in the outline.

The first nine MUSTS are self-explanatory. The "explanation, application, and motivation" in the tenth MUST needs further elaboration.

"Explanation"

As the Bible says, "The unfolding of Thy words gives light; / It gives understanding to the simple [unprejudiced (the original meaning in Greek)]" (Ps. 119:130). A teacher's paramount duty is to unfold God's Word to his students. If the unfolding of the passage is not thorough, then how can the students say "Amen"? The definition, sources, purposes, methods, and "don'ts" of explanation are described below.

(1) Definition:

Explanation means that a teacher uses questions and answers, illustrations, narrations, metaphors, idioms, detailed descriptions or even gestures to explain the content of a passage. These are essential to the students' understanding and recollection of God's Word, as well as the Holy Spirit's enlightenment regarding its reality.

(2) Sources of Explanation:

(a) The grammatical structure and accurate meaning of the passage in its original language (if possible).

(b) The biblical meaning applied in the passage (study the context of the passage).

(c) The historical, geographical, cultural, and traditional background of the passage.

(d) The principles of God's revelation (progressive and organic).

(e) The explicit and hidden meaning in the passage.

(f) The spiritual experiences of others or of your own.

(3) <u>Purposes of Explanation</u>:

(a) To make the content clear so that there is no ambiguity.

(b) To build up the main theme so that it is clear and obvious.

(c) To arouse the students' interest towards the lesson.

(d) To help students recall the lesson with ease.

(e) To enable students to be inspired more easily.

(f) To encourage students to apply the lesson.

(4) <u>Methods of Explanation</u>:

(a) Use words and phrases that are familiar to the students.

(b) Motivate students to think.

(c) Insert questions to get students involved.

(d) Explain new ideas (or insights) in detail.

(e) Explain according to the order of the verses, if possible.

(f) Apply the definition, analysis, comparison, and emphasis properly.

(g) Use illustrations appropriately.

(h) Use suitable tones, expressions, and gestures.

(i) Use audio-visual aids.

(j) Introduce books related to the lesson.

(5) <u>Don'ts of Explanation</u>:

(a) Don't explain what you do not thoroughly understand (especially the original language).

(b) Don't apply any explanation that is not completely accurate.

(c) Don't explain what cannot be explained.

(d) Don't waste time on what is unnecessary to explain.

(e) Don't over explain, but rather, conclude at the right point; don't "make a mountain out of a mole hill."

(f) Don't read from your outline; rather, elaborate from it.

(g) Don't use explanation to show off knowledge and to puff yourself up.

"Application"

Application means putting what has been learned into practice. God's truth is for our application, as the Bible says, "All Scripture is inspired [Greek: God-breathed]...that the man of God may be adequate, equipped for every good work" (2 Tim. 3:16-17). All Scripture is for us to put into practice right after hearing it. Therefore, Sunday school teaching should be neither empty talk nor lip service, else students may be at a loss, feeling powerless and frustrated towards the Bible. Pay attention to the following in "application":

(1) Definition:

Application is to prompt students to think and provide them with practical ways of applying what they have learned to their daily life. Application is also to instruct them about the required conditions that should be fulfilled and the steps that should be taken.

(2)   <u>Forms of Application</u>:

   (a)   Remarks: Use a few sentences to direct the students' attention to different areas in the passage that ought to be put into practice.

   (b)   Inference: Through inference, draw from the passage all that appeals to their emotions, and move the students to apply them willingly in their lives.

   (c)   Enlightenment: Through the prompting of insightful thoughts, strive to bring forth a more perfect and detailed enlightenment of the lesson that students may practice after class.

(3)   <u>Steps of Application</u>:

   (a)   Proposition: What should be applied? (content)

   (b)   Suggestion: How should it be applied or put into practice? (methods)

(c) Persuasion: Why should students apply or put it into practice? (reasons)

(4) <u>Purposes of Application</u>:

(a) To help students understand God's will.

(b) To put biblical truth into practice.

(c) To have optimal spiritual growth.

(d) To develop personal spiritual gifts.

(e) To be good examples to others.

(f) To lead others to the Lord.

(g) To speed up the coming of God's kingdom.

(5) <u>The Musts of Application</u>:

(a) It must immediately follow an explanation.

(b) It must be related closely to the actual daily lives of the students.

(c) It must be in harmony with the content of the lesson.

(d) It must encourage the students to march forward.

(e) It must correct the students' mistakes.

(f) It must be achievable by the students.

(g) It must be connected to the expansion of God's kingdom.

"Motivation"

If a teacher's lesson has explanation and application but not motivation (or incentive), it is just like a brand new car without an engine. Regardless of how splendidly it has been decorated, the car is in reality useless. This same analogy can be made concerning teaching Sunday school. A teacher not only has to explain the passage clearly and emphasize application, but also motivate students to apply and to put into practice what has been learned. Only then, will each student be as the Bible says, "one who. . .not having become a forgetful hearer but an effectual doer, this man shall be blessed in what he does" (Jas. 1:25). In "motivation," we should pay attention to the following:

(1) <u>Definition:</u>

Motivation is to stimulate students to enthusiastically, effectively and practically apply or put into practice the truths they have learned in their daily personal lives or work.

(2) <u>Purposes of Motivation:</u>

(a) To emphasize the importance of application.

(b) To remind students of the purpose of applying God's revelation.

(c) To strengthen the students' willingness to carry out the application.

(d) To encourage students to lay down themselves willingly for the Lord, in order to apply what they have learned.

(e) To motivate students to show empathy towards one another.

(3) <u>Factors of Motivation:</u>

(a) God's love.

(b) Commands of the Bible.

84

(c) Duties of a Christian.

(d) Needs of the world.

(e) Weakness of the Church today.

(f) Necessity for spiritual growth.

(g) Conditions for the Lord's second coming.

(4) <u>Methods of Motivation</u>:

(a) Challenge of the emotions.

(b) Persuasion of the intellect.

(c) Guidance of the will.

(d) Illumination of the Holy Spirit.

(5) <u>Suggestions for Motivation</u>:

(a) Pray for the motivation needed for your lesson.

(b) Be motivated by the passage yourself.

(c) Gradually achieve a climax in the progress of motivation, according to the development of the passage.

(d) Vary the words and phrases for motivation to avoid boredom.

(e) Use tones, gestures and pauses for emphasis.

(f) Use personal testimonies.

(g) Pray before and after the lesson for the power of motivation.

(h) Use illustrations and quotations from prominent and respected individuals.

(i) Use powerful Scripture passages.

(j) Suggest motivations subtly rather than through direct approaches.

It is inevitable that the above suggestions are incomplete. Because of the restriction imposed due to the length of this book, I can only touch on these principles briefly in the form of an outline. I do hope that Sunday school teachers are able to draw analogies from these suggestions, and with their own inferences, grasp a clear understanding of how a Sunday school lesson should be taught. By the grace of God, may all churches realize the importance of this ministry, that they will put Sunday school as their foremost priority, thereby establishing a solid reconstruction of the whole ministry. A strong Sunday school ministry will bring about the growth of the whole church, and will thus enable us to complete our gracious Lord's desire which He expressed in the Great Commission, "teaching them to observe all that I commanded you." Then, the Church will be blessed and God's kingdom will come all the sooner, "Amen! Come, Lord Jesus."

7

PRAY IN ONE ACCORD

The Church is the household of God, the Body of Christ and also the pillar and support of the Truth. Christ Himself built her (Matt. 16:18) and "purchased [her] with His own blood" (Acts 20:28).

In our Lord's discourse about the Church, however, He emphasized only the **authority** He gave to the Church: "Whatever you [the Church] bind on earth shall be bound in heaven; and whatever you [the Church] loose on earth shall be loosed in heaven" (Matt. 18:18). He never taught us the methods for establishing and expanding a church, nor the techniques for examining and training a Christian. Such omissions are effectively telling the Church this message of truth: If she is willing to utilize the authority given to her, and if she appropriates God's boundless riches, then the wisdom needed for church growth will certainly become her subjective wisdom instead of an objective knowledge. The Bible has said:

> If any of you lacks wisdom, let him **ask** of God, who gives to all men generously and without reproach....(Jas. 1:5)

Our Lord has even further promised that,

> ...if two of you agree on earth about anything that they may **ask**, it shall be done for them by My Father who is in heaven. For where two or three have gathered together in My name, there I am in their midst. (Matt. 18:19-20)

These promises are with conditions. If we desire our heavenly Father to answer our prayers or to be with us, a clear understanding of the following truths are a must.

The Plural Form Of "You"

The Roman Catholics have all along insisted that the "you" means the apostle Peter in Christ's statement:

> I will give **you** the keys of the kingdom of
> heaven; and whatever **you** shall bind on earth
> shall be bound in heaven, and whatever **you**
> shall loose on earth shall be loosed in heaven.
> (Matt. 16:19)

According to the context of this passage, we cannot deny that what they say is correct. But, the name "Peter" in this passage can possibly be the individual as well as a representation of the group.

God's revelation in the Bible is progressive; a later revelation usually clarifies an earlier one. The later revelation of this passage is found in Matt. 18:18:

> Truly I say to **you,** whatever **you** shall bind on
> earth shall be bound in heaven; and whatever
> **you** loose on earth shall be loosed in heaven.

Here the Bible uses the plural form of "you" ("to you"—plural; "you shall bind"—plural; and "you loose"—plural). It is clear then, from this latter revelation, that the pronoun "you" in Matthew 16:19 is not an individual but a representation of the whole. "Peter" is used to represent the whole Church!

To put it simply, our Lord has not bestowed on Peter, but on His own Church, the authority that binds and looses. His love for the Church allows her to be the one to initiate such an important decision on earth, as to "who should be bound and who should be loosed" in eternity; then our Father will pronounce the identical verdicts accordingly in heaven. On the other hand, if the Church on earth does not take any action, there will be complete "silence" in heaven. No wonder the prophet Isaiah says, "...You who remind the LORD, take no rest for yourselves; / And give Him no rest until He establishes and makes Jerusalem a praise in the earth" (Is. 62:6-7). If those on earth do not rest, He who is in heaven will not rest either. Hallelujah!

A Corporate Effort

People often say that it makes no difference whether you pray individually or with a group, nor does it matter whether you pray alone at home or together with brothers and sisters at church. Such a statement is merely a self-consolation of the lazy, or a plausible explanation of one ignorant of the power of prayer! See what our Lord says about this aspect of prayer:

> ...if two of you [Church] agree on earth about anything that they may ask....For where two or three have gathered together in My name....(Matt. 18:19-20)

Our Lord has emphatically reminded us that the utilization of this divine authority can never be achieved by the effort of one individual, but only through the corporate effort executed from the standpoint of the entire Church. In other words, only when Christians pray in one accord from the standpoint of the entire Church, can the Church then effectively use and enjoy such divine authority.

The Church of the last days, however, cannot see the reality of this truth, nor remember the proper procedure for the appropriation of God's power. What a great loss it is! She has the divine authority from heaven, but not the knowledge of its administration, yet she wants to bind the work of Satan, to loose the downtrodden, and to further experience the reality of God's presence. Alas, it cannot be done!

A Harmonious Chord

The Church has to practice reigning with Christ and having God's presence in order to grow. This dual blessing is attainable only when those who offer prayers have the correct perspective on their position, as well as a harmonious unity of their intent and attitude. Otherwise, laboring in vain is inevitable.

"In one accord" originally is a verb from which the English word "symphony" is translated. For a piece of music to be enjoyable and pleasing to the audience, every musician in an orchestra has to obey the conductor. In so doing, each note and each chord may be played harmoniously in one accord to produce an exquisite melody.

A prayer meeting is similar. There is only one difference between a symphony and a prayer meeting that reigns with Christ and has God's presence. The former desires the harmony of sounds, while the latter, the harmony of hearts! No wonder the Chinese Bible translates "in one accord" as "with the same heart and the same mind." Therefore, for a prayer meeting to have God's presence, not only must all participants understand the importance and the reality of prayer, but they must also come with a sincere desire to reign with God, and offer petitions, prayers, intercessions and thanksgivings to God in one accord. The prayer meeting will then be successful and other ministries will also operate smoothly. Praise the Lord!

An Uncompromising Faith

When our Lord was on the earth, He sighed and said, "When the Son of Man comes, will He find faith on the earth?" (Luke 18:8). This verse means, "When Christ comes to the world, it will be difficult to find anyone who has faith." The word "faith" has been widely used in the Bible. Its exact meaning can only be defined after a careful examination of its context. The text before this verse is the parable showing that we ought to pray at all times and not lose heart, while the text following is the parable of the prayers of a Pharisee and a tax collector. Thus, the context of this verse clearly indicates that the word "faith" here refers to the faith in prayer. And our Lord's statement is a lamentation that His Church will lose the faith of prayer on the eve of His second coming.

The prayer meetings of many churches today are actually deserted. Encountering such a sorrowful state, quite a number of churches totally ignore this important warning and in their indulgence for self-gratification, cancel their prayer meetings all together. It is truly the sign that the Lord's second coming is at hand! Nowadays, many Christians worship television more than their Lord who has delivered them from death into life. This is indeed sad!

There are two reasons why the churches of the last days exhibit such extreme apathy towards prayer meeting. These reasons are focused on Satan and the flesh.

a.   The restraints by Satan

Satan fully comprehends that the only means of prolonging his evil life is by delaying the second coming of Christ. If Satan devises a way of keeping the personnel of God's kingdom from being ready, Christ has to defer His coming. When the bride (the Church) is not ready, the groom (Christ) cannot come!

For this reason, he employs his evil schemes with all his might towards restraining people from believing in Jesus—thereby keeping the personnel of God's kingdom from being produced. By the grace of our Lord and the power of the Holy Spirit, many of the restrained are still able to obtain God's enlightenment and receive Jesus into their hearts, and thus are protected from the hand of the evil one. They have not only been "called" but may also have been "chosen."

Satan then starts the second step of his sabotage among these Christians, that is, restraining them from devoting time and effort in prayer. Satan knows (though Christians may not) that prayer is the procedure for the appropriation of God's riches in heaven. If Christians do not appropriate these riches, they will become exhausted spiritually and weakened prematurely. Consequently, they can never become the personnel for God's kingdom, and as a result, God's forthcoming kingdom is delayed. Therefore, the closer it is towards the eve of our Lord's second coming, the greater Satan's pressure will be against prayer!

Many pastors, evangelists and even seminary professors are falling under Satan's pressure so that they never pray after getting up in the morning! This situation will continue to worsen as time gets closer and closer to our Lord's coming. Unaware of Satan's control over them, these Christian leaders pridefully assume themselves as the spiritual pace-setters of their time. The result is both sorrowful and pitiful.

b. *The deceits of the flesh*

In the world there is nothing more deceitful than our flesh (Jer. 17:9). The Bible tells us:

> ...the flesh is hostile toward God; for it does
> not subject itself to the law of God, for it is not
> even able to do so....(Rom. 8:7)

Our flesh hates and opposes anything that is related to God, especially prayer meetings that work together with God. Therefore, it employs all its means and might to disrupt and paralyze such holy gatherings. The flesh is Satan's partner with a long-standing relationship and the two of them often collaborate to do evil. No matter whether it was to Adam, David, the Israelites or even to us today, if it had not been for the help of the flesh, Satan could never have offered his temptations.

Our constant alertness towards man's deceitful nature has protected us from the harm of many frauds; but our relaxation towards the flesh has led us into many snares. For instance, we may feel light-headed when we first get up in the morning. With self-pity and compassion, we immediately decide, "Never mind! I will pray to God at noon!" When noon comes, we are busy about this and so concerned about that, that we think we can wait until the evening to say our prayers. In the evening, after a day of hard work, we are totally exhausted, so we console ourselves and say, "God understands. He does not mind!" Yes, God does not mind; but for a whole long day, we carried on without the appropriation of God's grace. It is our great loss.

The deferment of personal morning prayers is the starting point of backsliding and failure for many Christians. It is also the very first step of "falling away from the living God" for many Christians.

Years ago when I was preaching at a church in Hong Kong, a wealthy sister (who is with the Lord now) came to me after the meeting and confessed this: "Many a time I would rather spend one or two days preparing a meal for my friends, than devote three minutes in prayer for them!" "To hate work, but to love pleasure" is natural. However, when we come to spiritual matters related to God, we would rather substitute pleasure with work, that is—"To hate prayer, but to love work." How strange it is! Such a reaction towards God is the nature of the flesh: "As long as I can act against God, I do not mind to work a little bit harder." May God open our eyes that we may truly know how our flesh works.

There was another incident. One day, the coordinator of the Ministers' Prayer Meeting (of a certain city in North America) telephoned a pastor to remind him of the prayer meeting on that following Monday evening. It happened that the pastor was out and his wife answered the phone. After learning the purpose of the call, that pastor's wife cursed the coordinator, saying, "In this age, you people still pray, pray, pray! You're wasting your time! You should hasten to work..." She thought that praying was a waste of time! It is no wonder that soon after every appointment as pastor of a church, that pastor and his wife had to move on to another church. Pastors who do not depend on our mighty God, but on their own limited wisdom, will forever be "job-hopping."

Dear brothers and sisters, please keep in mind that participation in regular church prayer meetings is a condition for maintaining God's presence. A church that has a beautifully blooming prayer meeting, will never be in the midst of a heavy snow storm at the same time. On the other hand, negligence of prayer will cost us God's presence, and thus, all efforts put forth will either be striving after the wind or grasping for shadows. In the end, there is nothing. May God have mercy upon us.

A Serious Practice

The tabernacle and the holy temple in the Old Testament are types of Christ. It is recorded in the Gospel of John:

> And the Word became flesh [flesh tabernacled (in Greek)], and dwelt among us....(John 1:14)

> Jesus answered and said to them, "Destroy this temple, and in three days I will raise it up."... He [Jesus] was speaking of the temple of His body. (John 2:19-21)

At the same time, the tabernacle and the holy temple (especially the holy temple), are also types of the Church. It is written in the New Testament:

> Do you [the Church] not know that you [the Church] are a temple of God...for the temple of God is holy, and that is what you are. (1 Cor. 3:16-17)

> ...in whom the whole building, being fitted together is growing into a holy temple in the Lord....(Eph. 2:21)

Christ and the Church in fact belong to the same body—Christ "is also the head of the body, the Church" (Col. 1:18), and the Church "is His body" (Eph. 1:23). How wonderful and glorious it is!

Inside the holy temple, in front of the ark of the covenant within the holy of holies, there is a golden altar of incense. This golden altar is a type of Church prayer meeting because the incense burned on the altar represents "the prayers of the saints" (Psalm 141:2; Rev. 5:8; 8:4). A church that has no prayer meeting is like the holy temple without a golden altar.

God Himself taught Moses the special method of preparing this incense, as well as its application. We can meditate on these three aspects: the ingredients, the preparation, and the functions of the incense (Ex. 30:34-38).

a. The ingredients of the incense

There are four ingredients for making the incense: stacte, onycha, galbanum and pure frankincense. In the lapse of time, we no longer have any good knowledge of what these spices are, except for pure frankincense. The quality of these ingredients, however, must be pure and of a soothing aroma, because our Holy God wants an offering with a soothing aroma (Lev. 1:9, 13, 17). No wonder that a prayer with impurities is impossible to please God (Is. 59:1-2). Although we have no idea what the other three Old Testament incense ingredients really are, we can see in the New Testament what all four of them represent. They represent four different kinds of prayer: petition (deēsis), prayer (proseuchē), intercession (enteuxis) and thanksgiving (eucharistia)(1 Tim. 2:1-2).

"Petition"

Although from its connotation, especially in vernacular Greek, this word means "entreaty" or "supplication," yet in reality it is almost the same as prayer and intercession. In the New Testament, however, it often means "to concentrate on petitions" or "to pray earnestly." For instance, in the passage where Jesus "offered up both prayers and supplications with loud crying and tears" in the garden of Gethsemane, it is in fact, Jesus "offered up both petitions and entreaties" in the Greek original (Heb. 5:7). In another passage where Anna "never left the temple, serving night and day with fastings and prayers," the word "petition" is used in the original language instead of "prayer" (Luke 2:37). In the passage concerning spiritual warfare, we not only have to pray with all "prayer" but also with all "petition" (Eph. 6:18). And, in the promise that

"The effective prayer of a righteous man can accomplish much," the word "prayer" is actually "petition" in Greek as well (Jas. 5:16).

Oftentimes our prayers lack spiritual power. Perhaps, it is because they are just empty slogans that mean nothing, except that the failure to practice is a dereliction of Christian duty. A spiritual brother perpetually having deep insights concerning God, once said, "If our own hearts are not moved by our prayers, how can we then expect God's heart to be moved?"

"Prayer"

This word appears 37 times as a noun and 87 times as a verb in the New Testament. When the intent is to emphasize on the need for prayer, the word "petitions" or phrases like "devoting yourselves to," "fervently," "with all" or "be on the alert," are often used in conjunction with the word "prayer." It is crucial to devote oneself to fervent prayer with great concentration for a particular need, but it is also vital to have regular prayer. We ought to pray regularly every day or every week for all our needs. A pastor in particular has to pray regularly (every day or every week) in an orderly manner for all the needs of his church. If some urgent matter comes up in the church, he then has to devote himself to fervent prayer with great concentration.

"Intercession"

This word appears only two times in the New Testament in Greek (1 Tim. 2:1 and 1 Tim. 4:5). Some Christians oppose the practice of having one person say grace for a group of Christians, because they hold the view that each Christian should say grace individually. According to 1 Timothy 4:5, however, God's revelation is for one person to say grace and the others to respond with "Amen." The original meaning of "intercession" is "to talk with confidence, without cringing or apprehension." In vernacular Greek its meaning also includes the submission of a written statement or a petition to his emperor. The connotation of this word clearly indicates that we should be bold in our intercession for all men, especially for kings and those in authority, because God is pleased with our intercession. In the Old Testament, God expressed His extreme astonishment that "there was no man—no one to intercede" in Israel! Does He have the same lamentation about our church today—"there was [is] no man...no one to intercede"?

And He saw that there was no man,
And was astonished that there was no one to
intercede; (Is. 59:16)

"Thanksgiving"

The word "thanksgiving" has appeared 15 times in the New Testament. Its original meaning is "matters to be thankful for," and the word Holy Communion comes from this word. Therefore, Holy Communion is "a matter to be thankful for."

In 1983 the topic for the Chinese composition for the Taiwan College Entry Joint Examination was "Respect Yourself, Care for Others"; and for the High School Entry Examination, "Please, Thank You, Sorry!" Chinese are famous for concealing deep feelings. Though overwhelmed with gratitude and appreciation, expressing verbal thankfulness is oftentimes difficult. As we enter into our new found Christian faith, we often bring with us this same unexpressive, imprudent subtlety which ill-treats God and harms ourselves. To say "thank you" to relatives and friends for any favor or gift received is a teaching we always remind our children, but forget to train ourselves, especially in thanking our Father in heaven. For this reason the Bible reminds us to keep "alert...with an attitude of thanksgiving" (Col. 4:2). At times we must admit that our prayers are indeed filled with petitions and intercessions, but lack thanksgivings. God's charge to us is to be alert to all matters that we ought to be thankful for, lest we fall short in our thanksgivings to our blessed Lord.

The best way of keeping alert in another person's prayer or thanksgiving is to softly follow the prayer and respond with "Amen" (1 Cor. 14:16).

Spiritual maturity and godly virtues cannot be achieved by merely heeding a few sermons, but through the accumulation of months and years of earnest, painstaking practice. Thanksgiving is no exception. Only through continuous practice can we be the ones who "pray without ceasing" and "in everything give thanks" (1 Thess. 5:17-18).

b.   The preparation of the incense

God has a patent for the incense formula which no one should reproduce. If anyone desires to reproduce any incense like this for his own enjoyment, he will meet God's severe judgment. In Exodus 30:37-38 God has clearly stated:

> ...you shall not make in the same proportions for yourselves; it shall be holy to you for the LORD. Whoever shall make any like it, to use as perfume, shall be cut off from his people.

This incense represents "the prayers of the saints" (Ps. 141:2; Rev. 5:8; 8:4). From a study of the incense preparations, we can derive some spiritual insights as to how our prayers should be practiced.

"To salt it"

In order for the incense to become pure and holy, aside from the four ingredients previously described, salt is needed. Salt has two meanings in the Bible. It represents God's faithfulness and trustworthiness, because the covenant He made with the Israelites was a covenant of salt— symbolizing the permanency and incorruptibility of the covenant (Num. 18:19). It is also an indispensable requirement of a successful prayer— to be at peace with others.

Our Lord's commandment is, "Have salt in yourselves, and be at peace with one another" (Mark 9:50). Unless there is complete trust in God and absolute peace with others, our prayers will be in vain. In the kingdom prayer, our Lord neither emphasizes the kingdom nor His will, but presses home the requirement that protects our prayer. It is, "And forgive us our debts, as we also have forgiven our debtors" (Matt. 6:12)—that is, to be at peace with others. This essential point has not only been mentioned twice in the constitution of the kingdom (Matt. 5:23-26; 6:14-15), but also with dual emphasis each time. In the Bible, when God wants to press home a certain truth, He always uses either a negative command (Matt. 7:6) or an affirmative order (Matt. 7:7) to stress its importance. In Matthew Chapter 6, however, He first emphasizes with the affirmative (6:14) and then with the negative (6:15). The paramount importance of "being at peace with others" in relationship to prayer is evident.

At the beginning of our faith, when we confess our sins and believe in Christ, our sins are forgiven. But after becoming a Christian, there is a condition for the confession of sins: "If we do not forgive others, then our Father will not forgive our transgressions"! May God help us to forgive others, lest our prayers be hindered and our church be hampered from growth.

"To beat it very fine"

This second step of preparation explains why sometimes our prayers are not answered. Perhaps they are too sketchy. The prayers that God wants are those abundant in detail. The preparation word "fine" is equivalent to the New Testament's "with all prayer and petition" as stated in Paul's letter to the Ephesians (Eph. 6:18). God desires us to cast upon Him every aspect and concern for each prayer item, instead of merely naming our need. By praying for each aspect in detail, our front line defense on the spiritual battlefield will then be flawless and unbreachable. On the other hand, God's power is likened to electricity and our prayers, to an electric wire. When there is a wire, electricity will follow wherever the wire leads. The action from heaven is the same. God's power will follow our prayers on earth. The lack of manifestation of God's power in a certain ministry is because our prayers lack fineness in that ministry.

If we merely name our prayer items absent-mindedly, how can we expect our Father in heaven to listen attentively? Perhaps some may say, "How about the tax collector in Luke Chapter 18? Wasn't his short prayer answered?" Yes, it was. But please also study David's confession in Psalm 51, and Daniel's confession in Daniel Chapter 9. After reading these three confessions, which one has blessed you most? Furthermore, have not Solomon's prayer for the dedication of the holy temple (1 Kin. 8:23-61) and Christ's prayer for the unity of His disciples (John 17:1-26) told us that prayer has to be "fine"?

c.   *The functions of the incense*

God has said, "put part of it [the incense] before the testimony in the tent of meeting, where I shall meet with you..." (Ex. 30:36). In the Old Testament, God and man meet in front of the testimony, for it is here that the radiance of God's glory shines from the mercy seat on top of the testimony. This radiance represents the Lord Jesus who is "the radiance of His glory" (Heb. 1:3) and only in Him there is true "Emmanuel" (Ex. 30:36). That is why we have to pray in the name of Jesus (John 14:14).

The general goal for prayer is asking God's consent to bless us with His grace, to heal the sick, to comfort the downhearted, to provide for the needy, to deliver those in trial, to help unbelievers believe and believers grow, and so on. In fact, all these requests are cures for the symptoms rather than for the root of the problem. Our Lord has already given us the cure for the root of the problem—His presence with us!

With His presence, all these problems will be resolved, darkness will turn to light, and calamity will become riches. That is the reason why He said in the Old Testament,

> And you shall beat some of it very fine, and put part of it before the testimony in the tent of meeting, where I shall meet with you.... (Ex. 30:36)

and in the New Testament,

> For where two or three have gathered together in My name, there I am in their midst. (Matt. 18:20)

Praise the Lord! He has promised to be with us through prayer. If we are willing to carry out the condition He ordered, the promise of His presence will then be fully realized among us. Hallelujah!

The goal of prayer is to have God's presence. If our prayer is for our own enjoyment and the satisfaction of our lusts, how can we then have God's presence? This is what James says, "You ask and do not receive, because you ask with wrong motives, so that you may spend it on your pleasures" (Jas. 4:3).

CONCLUSION

The Church, according to God's design, should exercise leadership in the world; she should be "the leader, rather than the follower" and "on the top, rather than at the bottom" of society. But, in reality, the Church today is the exact opposite of that purpose. She is not only incapable of leading society, but is also eager to follow each and every one of its worldly trends. Of course, she can never catch up with this world and has, therefore, often become an object of scorn in the world. It is sad indeed!

Christians of all ages have sincerely desired growth in God's Church. In the 1970s and 1980s especially, the call for church growth resounded throughout the whole world. Movements of church growth received enthusiastic response everywhere. However, substantial church growth remains remote!

The law of causality dictates that everything has its cause and effect—no effect can exist apart from its cause, and no cause can exist apart from its effect. Perhaps, the present state of the Church is a result of her being apart from her "cause"! This book is an attempt to search for her "cause." It is hoped that on the eve of our Lord's second coming His Church can rediscover the "cause" of church growth, that the "effect" of growth may be in full blossom everywhere.

The conditions required for church growth and God's presence are, of course, far more than those mentioned in this book, but, in this space age where simplicity and time are of top priority, the seven chapters of this book may have already been too complicated and too long.

A person's conscientiousness in his work and the achievements in his career are often in direct proportion. Likewise, especially in the ministry of church growth, we should never be sidetracked from the core of the matter by dwelling on minor points (selected according to our own liking), but should ceaselessly seek God's presence. We have to forsake, repudiate and break through anything that impedes God's presence, regardless of the seriousness of its damage and the power of its resistance. On the other hand, we must try our best to pursue, execute and lay down ourselves for any condition that brings forth God's presence, regardless of the cost and sacrifice. Then, the God of peace Himself will surely be with the Church, and He will help her carry out the Great Commission with which He has entrusted her.

"Amen. Come, Lord Jesus!"

BIOGRAPHICAL NOTES

Dr. Timothy Lin was born to a minister's family in Chekiang, China, and came to a saving knowledge of our Savior Jesus Christ at the age of 19. After seminary training, Dr. Lin's early years of ministry included pastoral and administrative duties in Shanghai and Kwangsi respectively. However, theological education in China was very superficial. Consequently, he came to the United States to study Hebrew and Greek in 1940.

During the difficult years of World War II, he served the Lord in Shanghai as head of an orphanage, principal of a high school and dean of a Bible college. After the war, he was called to be president of East China Theological College in Hangchow. In 1948, he returned to the U.S. for advanced studies, and earned Master degrees in Divinity and Sacred Theology from Faith Theological Seminary (then in Delaware), and a Ph.D. in Old Testament Hebrew from the College of Hebrew and Cognate Learnings at Dropsie University. He then taught in the Graduate School of Bob Jones University, South Carolina.

For over fifty years, Dr. Lin has devoted his life to the study and teaching of God's Word, and has been God's faithful servant in the First Chinese Baptist Church of Los Angeles since 1961. In addition to his busy pastoral duties, he has taught at Talbot Seminary in Los Angeles and Trinity Evangelical Seminary in Chicago. He was a member of the translation team for the Old Testament section of the New American Standard Bible. From 1980 to 1990, he served as president of China Evangelical Seminary in Taiwan.

During the past thirty years, Dr. Lin has traveled extensively to preach and teach at different churches in many parts of Asia, North America, Australia and Europe. His burden for lost souls throughout the world has motivated him to train and equip Christians to become personnel of God's kingdom.

Many Christians and church leaders have been richly blessed in the past by his wisdom, teaching, leadership and example. He is more than a scholar of God's Word, for God has given him authority and power to speak for Him.